JUÁREZ

A Son of the People

JUÁREZ

A Son of the People

4654

by JEAN ROUVEROL

CROWELL-COLLIER PRESS, New York, New York
COLLIER-MACMILLAN PUBLISHERS, LONDON

Frontispiece: Painting of Juárez by Diego Rivera;
photo Historical Pictures Service—Chicago

The Macmillan Company, 866 Third Avenue, New York, N.Y. 10022
Collier-Macmillan Canada Ltd., Toronto, Ontario

Library of Congress catalog card number: 72-81071

Printed in the United States of America

10 9 8 7 6 5 4 3 2 1

"Among nations, as among individuals, respect for the rights of others is peace."—*Benito Juárez*

CONTENTS

JUÁREZ
A Son of the People

1

BEGINNINGS

San Pablo Guelatao
1806-1818

High in the Sierra del Sur above the valley of Oaxaca, March was three quarters over. Here and there above the valley a cone thrust upward amid the chaotic mountains to show the land's volcanic origin. Pinewoods shadowed the slopes, and deep, dry arroyos dropped suddenly away, waiting till the rainy season should turn them into muddy torrents. In one of the tiny Indian villages whose inhabitants lived not too differently from the Zapotecs of a thousand years ago, Brigida García de Juárez delivered another baby. A boy.

Marcelino Juárez and his wife were as obscure as any Indian couple toiling for a living in those inhospitable mountains. For thousands of years, Zapotec Indians had lived, and borne their babies, and died, in the sierra and in the valley of Oaxaca below. They were a stocky, dark-skinned people with high, wide cheekbones. Sober and hard-working, with a profound sense of honor, they bore even their poverty with dignity.

The Zapotecs had resisted the Aztec invasion from the north longer than any of the other Indian tribes of Mexico. In the sixteenth century, when the rest of Mexico had succumbed in superstitious terror before the invading Spaniards—or had put up only a brief and hopeless resistance—it had cost the Spanish generals three expeditions to subdue these people of the Oaxacan plains and mountains. They were not warlike, but they were stubborn, and they fought for what was rightfully theirs.

This, then, was the heritage of the newborn Zapotec baby. If he could survive the onslaughts of disease—smallpox, yellow fever, cholera—which regularly decimated the Indians of southern Mexico, and if he did not die of starvation, he still had little to look forward to except a life of isolation, poverty, and complete anonymity. Certainly in this obscure and mountainous region, whose people were almost entirely illiterate, one more Indian baby couldn't count for much.

Nevertheless, on March 22, when the baby was one day old, his father, his godmother, and his grandparents toiled up the mountain to the village of Santo Tomás Ixtlán, where there was a little church. There the baby's birth was recorded, and he was baptized Pablo Benito Juárez.

Within three years he was left with neither mother nor father. Brigida had died giving birth to a little girl; and Marcelino, who one day had walked the forty miles down the mountain to the city of Oaxaca to sell fruit, dropped dead in the halls of the municipal palace. Benito and his baby sister were orphans.

But Indian families are endlessly flexible. The two children's grandparents and their older sisters, María Josefa and Rosa, took care of them. Within a few years more, however, the grandparents too had died. María Josefa and Rosa, as young women will, got married. Now who would look after the two small orphans? In all the village of San Pablo Guelatao there were only twenty families, hardly a hundred people. Who could afford to feed two more mouths?

There was an aunt to take Benito's little sister. And Benito himself was taken in by one of his father's brothers, Bernardino Juárez, who could boast a small herd of sheep and a little piece of ground near the Laguna Encantada, the Enchanted Lake.

It was not much of a life for a small boy. Uncle Bernardino was hard-pressed by poverty and the demands of his land and his herd. He had no time to waste looking after his orphaned nephew, and Benito soon learned what ill treatment was, and neglect. When he was old enough to think for himself, he was sent out into the fields to help with the farm work, and eventually his uncle turned over to him the tending of the sheep.

There was the lake, of course. It was ringed by trees, and there was reputed to be a water witch living under its waters. Years later a legend was told in Guelatao that Benito had fallen asleep on a clump of bushes by the lake's edge and had wakened at night to find himself adrift on the angry waters amid a terrible storm, with rain pummeling down and lightning flashing. Not until morning, when the storm died, was the boy able to get his perilous bark to shore. People of the area have told and retold this story, to prove that fate was protecting Benito because it had something more in mind for him than drowning in an enchanted lake.

Meanwhile, he grew hardy, as boys do who live outdoors and work constantly. He became rugged, his short frame grew muscular. Reserved to the point of shyness, he was alone most of the time and learned to depend on himself. He made a few friends, however, who learned to respect him for his sober good judgment. Their word for him was "formal," which in the Mexican sense means he was scrupulous about meeting every obligation.

And sometimes a passing relative would find him stationed in a tree, haranguing his herd of sheep in the Zapotec language. In Zapotec, because Benito could not speak Spanish. Nor, indeed, could the majority of Indians in that remote and mountainous part of Mexico.

It seemed, in those years, that he would pass his life like the other boys of his village: tending the sheep, farming, making charcoal to sell in the market, speaking only his local dialect and never the language of his country. He would grow up, father children, and die in the sierra, leaving no evidence that he had ever existed, except for one or two entries in the register of an obscure parish church and finally, perhaps, a tombstone in the parish churchyard, or an unmarked grave on the pine-covered hillside above his village.

But Uncle Bernardino, whose life was wearing away in just such weary anonymity, gave Benito one piece of wisdom: *he must get an education.* If he could learn to speak Spanish and to read it, he could perhaps study to become a priest, because even a poor Indian boy could aspire to the priesthood. This much, at least, was open to him.

"These promptings," Benito was to write years later, ". . . awoke in me a vehement desire to learn." His uncle even tried, in the few moments of leisure left him after the day's toil, to teach him to read. Benito's eagerness was so great that when he was called to his lesson, "I myself brought him the whip to punish me if I did not know it."

But uncle and nephew were both so involved in their endless round of drudgery that Benito made little progress.

There was one other path open to the boy. Parents up in the sierra who dreamed of a better life for their children sometimes took them down to the valley, to the city of Oaxaca, and put them into service as domestics in private homes, on condition that they be taught to read and write. Most of the households in Oaxaca had such youngsters as servants. Benito begged his uncle to take him down to the city. But Bernardino, perhaps because he needed Benito's help with the sheep, or perhaps because of a grudging affection he felt for his nephew, postponed a decision. He didn't refuse outright. He merely said he'd take him *some* day.

But "some day" did not come, and time was going by. Benito was twelve years old. For all his desperate conviction that he must go to Oaxaca and get an education, it seemed as though he would grow to adulthood and spend the rest of his life in the sierra, eking a bare living out of that mountainous soil.

It was December 16, 1818. Four days before, the little village had celebrated Guadalupe Day, the day of Mexico's patron saint, the Virgin of Guadalupe. Benito was in the fields watching the sheep when some muleteers came by, on their way farther up into the mountains. Benito discovered they had come from Oaxaca and engaged them in a conversation, asking them about the city. But when the strangers had gone their way, he discovered how costly the few words had been. One of his uncle's sheep was missing, taken by the muleteers.

Benito knew only too well what his uncle would do to him when the loss was discovered, and he thought of running away. But this was the only home he could re-

member, and for all his harshness, his uncle had been
generous in sheltering him when he was an orphan and
alone. Benito was also reluctant, as he later wrote, ". . .
to abandon my friends, toward whom I had always felt
the deepest warmth, and from whom any separation always wounded me. The conflict I felt between these
emotions, and the desire to go to a new and strange society where I could get an education, was cruel indeed."

Nevertheless, his fear of his uncle's anger and his desire for an education outweighed all else. At dawn the
following morning he slipped out of the slumbering village and began the forty-mile walk down the mountains
to the city of Oaxaca.

2

LEARNING

Oaxaca
1818-1828

It was long after twilight when Benito reached the outskirts of the city. The dark streets were unfamiliar to
him. He had never so much as seen a city before. But
somehow, speaking only his native Zapotec and knowing
only that his sister worked in the household of a don
Antonio Maza, he made his way to the house where
María Josefa was employed.

There he was taken in, and only a twelve-year-old boy
who has walked forty miles down a mountainside can
know how weary he must have been that night, how
hungry and thirsty, how bedraggled the white cotton
calzones he wore as trousers, and how blistered and sore
his feet in their dusty sandals. The *petate*, the straw mat
spread out on the cement floor of the Maza servants'
room, must have seemed a welcome bed indeed.

Daytime revealed to him a city which Mexico's Spanish conquerors had built with loving care. It was a city of graceful colonial houses in pastel colors, wrought-iron grillwork at window and gateway, pink and scarlet bougainvillea climbing the walls, and a multitude of trees in the plazas. Within the enclosed patios were orange, and Indian laurel, purple jacaranda, bamboo, and the wide, rich green leaves of banana trees. And on the streets and in the teeming market were dark-skinned Indians like himself, who had come down from the sierra to sell their goods, or from the poorer sections of the city where they lived. They spoke Mixtec or Zapotec, and were altogether in curious contrast to the affluence of the city.

While Benito looked for a household job, he was put to work taking care of señor Maza's cochineal, insects which provided the red pigment used to dye Oaxaca's hand-loomed cloth. During all of Mexico's life as a Spanish colony, cochineal and indigo had been almost the only exports the mother country allowed her, because they did not compete with Spain's own industries.

Benito worked thus for his keep until he was hired as a houseboy in the home of don Antonio Salanueva. Salanueva was a bookbinder, and a lay brother of the Third Order of St. Francis. Although deeply religious, he was an extraordinarily broad-minded man, passionately dedicated to young people's education. His house was dark and small, with the bookbindery in front, just off the street, but Salanueva's library and the multitude of books among which he worked must have seemed to Benito like a wonderland. The gentle and pious man became much more than Benito's employer. He adopted him. For the first time in his conscious memory, the all-but-illiterate boy knew what it was to have a father.

Don Antonio's first act was to put Benito into an elementary school. Here he learned reading and writing and the catechism, but nothing at all of Spanish grammar. The teaching was poor, and the children of the class, like Benito, spoke only their native dialects. By the time Benito was in fourth grade he was still barely able to write the language of his country.

This was not what he had traveled so far to find. He asked to be transferred to another school, where both Indians and the sons of some of the wealthier families studied. In a school that taught the sons of "respectable" families, one could surely acquire Spanish!

But once within the walls of the Royal School, he learned otherwise.

He was shown into a class made up of *inditos*, young Indians like himself, while the well-dressed, well-to-do boys were taught by the maestro in another part of the school. The assistant who conducted Benito's class handed him an assignment, and Benito set to work, laboring over it till the end of the day.

His teaching up to now had not prepared him for ordinary fourth-grade work. He was aware that his lesson was full of errors, but he hoped the assistant would help him correct them. The assistant, however, lost his temper and ordered Benito punished for his mistakes in grammar.

Benito had not met injustice before. He smarted over it now, doubly so because the "respectable" boys in the other part of the school were being taught by a qualified teacher, one who was far less lavish with his punishments.

What to do? "I decided," he wrote later, "to leave school and practice by myself the little I had learned, until I could express my ideas in writing—however poor the form might be, as it is to this day."

From then on, at the end of each day's chores, he sat up far into the night, reading, scribbling, and studying. For a time, his only light was a piece of rosin given him by a woman in the neighboring courtyard. For years, this was all the education that his promised land, Oaxaca, provided him.

All was not work, however. Somehow, squeezed in between his self-imposed studies, his household chores, and the religious observances his foster father insisted on, Benito found time for escapades with other boys his age. They tried constructing a springboard at a lake where they swam. They ran, jumped (one heroic jump landed him in the gutter and got him a whipping for wetting his clean clothes), and sometimes pelted passers-by with apples.

To the west of the city, the moss-grown ruins of Monte Alban crowned the green-brown hills, mute testimony to the greatness of two thousand years of Zapotec culture.

But Benito's friends noticed that he seemed more interested in the condition of the Indians he could see on the streets about him, or in the market. "When I have money," he declared, "I shall give it to that poor man—and some day, I shall have it!"

For some time, he had been aware of the young men going to and from the local religious seminary, studying for the priesthood. He had also noticed the respect with which these students were treated by the townspeople. Not that he wanted to become a priest—far from it. But he remembered his uncle's advice: here was a chance for advancement, even for an Indian. So, one quiet moment at the bookbindery, he took the matter up with Salanueva, promising that he would still manage to take care of his household duties if only he were allowed to study at the seminary.

Salanueva was delighted. In spite of Benito's admission that he did not want to become a priest, Salanueva undoubtedly thought the boy would change his mind. So, in October, 1821, Benito entered the seminary for a two-year study of Latin grammar, before he had properly learned Spanish.

At the end of two years, he had passed his examinations with distinction. The question was, what now? He knew Latin, but not much else, and there was a course in arts and philosophy open to him which he longed to enter. Or, he could take up a course with the forbidding title, "Moral Philosophy," which would prepare him for immediate entry into the priesthood. This, of course, was don Antonio's wish.

But not Benito's. Oaxaca and the surrounding villages teemed with parish priests who had studied only Latin grammar and moral philosophy. They were referred to scornfully as "priests of mass and stew" because they could earn only the meagerest livelihood by saying mass; they were considered too ignorant to preach or do anything else which required learning and ability. The thought of such a life for himself, Benito wrote years later, "was deeply repugnant to me."

He explained this to his godfather, and pleaded that in any event he was still too young to become a priest. So the gentle bookbinder let him have his way. Benito would study art and philosophy.

By the time he was twenty-one he had completed this course, too, with consistently good grades from the seminary. There was no putting it off any longer. He must repay his obligation to Salanueva and study moral philosophy, to prepare himself for a career as a humble parish priest.

Though he would not be quite as anonymous as his fellow Indians who never ventured down from the sierra, his would still be a life of limited usefulness and little respect. He had come some distance, this young Zapotec, but not far enough.

However, in 1828, by the time he had fulfilled his godfather's wishes and completed his religious training,

something had happened in Mexico, and in the state of
Oaxaca, that gave new hope and new opportunity to
young Indians like Benito. Now, perhaps, he would have
a chance to see beyond the encircling hills to farther
horizons.

3

"NEW SPAIN"
AND INDEPENDENCE

1519-1827

Three centuries before, in 1519, a brilliant, ruthless Spaniard named Hernando Cortés had landed his ships at the island of San Juan de Ulúa, in the harbor of Veracruz on the Caribbean, with five hundred men, ten cannon, and a few more than a dozen horses. He burned his ships to make sure there could be no retreat. Then, on the mainland, he subdued the local Indians and pressed forward to challenge the mighty Aztecs in the valley of Mexico.

The Aztecs had a thriving empire. They were a warlike people who practiced human sacrifice. The Spaniards, in the name of their own empire and their religion, were equally bloody and considerably more sophisticated. Cortés took an Indian mistress named Malinche, and using her as his interpreter, conquered many tribes by guile. Others he decimated with his guns. He was inexhaustible. When his supply of gunpowder was used up, he lowered one of his soldiers down the crater of the still-smoldering volcano Popocatepetl to scrape sulphur from its sides. Nothing could halt his march toward total conquest.

Within a few years it was all over. The Spaniards had imposed their language, their culture, and their religion on the captive peoples. The gentle Zapotecs and Mixtecs of Oaxaca were deceived into submission, and within a generation, says one writer, "Reports sent to the King of Spain show an almost incredible slaughter of the population—by plagues introduced from Europe, by overwork, but mostly by sorrow. Almost every old town was reduced to a fourth of its former size, and others were mere skeletons. . . . The people were drinking, which they had never done before—but they had never been unhappy before."

The Spaniards mined the gold and silver from Mexico's mountains and sent it back to Spain by the shipload, depleting forever Mexico's natural wealth. They forbade the growing of crops which might compete with those of the mother country—wine grapes, for instance, flax and hemp, olives, and the mulberry tree, needed for the production of silk. And they placed so many regulations on her manufacture, and such heavy taxes on her trade, that her industry was all but crippled. The Franciscan fathers took pity on the Indians and established schools for them, but over the years the padres' interest waned, and most of the schools died out. Slavery was supposedly illegal, but it existed. Peons working on the vast haciendas accumulated debts to their masters. When they died these debts passed to their sons, so countless Indians, one generation after another, were trapped in a kind of debt slavery.

By the time of Juárez's birth, Indians made up four-fifths of the population of Mexico and were in considerably worse condition than they had been at the time of the conquest. Many had been reduced by debt to peonage on the great ranching or mining haciendas. They had to pay tithes to the church and enormous fees to the priests for every major event of their lives, baptism, marriage, funeral. Most of them were illiterate, and none were allowed any position of importance in the church, nor in government, law, or medicine.

But the rebellion, when it began, did not originate with the Indians. It was sparked by the Creoles, men of Spanish blood born in the New World. The Creoles were allowed no part in the government of Mexico, and they bitterly resented it. Equally angry and restless were the mestizos, those people of mixed Indian and Spanish heritage.

Both Creoles and mestizos had enough education to know that the world was stirring, that the American colonists and the French working classes had rebelled against oppression, that Napoleon Bonaparte, in his military sweep, had upset the oldest ruling dynasties of Europe, including that of Spain.

The fateful year for Mexico, and indeed for all of Spanish America, was 1810.

In that year Benito Juárez had turned four years old and he and his baby sister were newly orphaned. In the quiet, slow-moving life of his mountain village, an uprising hundreds of miles to the north must have seemed as distant as if it had occurred on another planet. But before a score of years was out, the events set in motion one September day in Querétaro would change not only Benito's life, but the lives of all his countrymen.

It began prematurely. The little group of conspirators in and around Querétaro had not considered they were quite ready to begin their fight for freedom. But a would-be rebel, a member of the army stationed there, became frightened at his complicity and confessed all to his commanding officer, naming as one of the ringleaders a local Creole aristocrat, Ignacio Allende. Someone reached Allende to warn him, and Allende rode that night to the village of Dolores to alert his fellow conspirator, Father Miguel Hidalgo. The two leaders were advised to flee at once, but Hidalgo refused even to consider the idea.

Hidalgo was a gentle, elderly parish priest who had dreamed of some sort of cooperative society for his parishioners. He had introduced potteries, tanneries, beehives, and (strictly against the law) flax, slikworms, olive groves, vineyards and distilleries into his district, that his Indians might grow in skills and wealth. Then the Spaniards had come to Dolores and cut down his trees and vines, which no doubt fired Hidalgo's conviction that the only hope for his Indians lay in freedom from Spain.

The elderly padre was a man of impulse, and his impulses were sometimes inspired—but not always. That night of September 15, he acted promptly, moving his men out into the sleeping village and bundling every influential Spaniard, priest or merchant, off to prison. By dawn of the sixteenth the rebels were firmly in control of the town, and at midmorning Hidalgo made the famous *grito*—cry—to the people of Dolores, that they must march for freedom in the name of America and the Virgin of Guadalupe.

March they did, thousands of Indians and mestizos armed with clubs, axes, knives, machetes, and, like David facing Goliath, slings. In San Miguel troops guarding the public plaza broke ranks and joined the rebels. As they marched, they drew more recruits. Before long they were an army, ragged and ill equipped, but fifty thousand strong.

At Guanajuato the Spanish commandant abandoned the townspeople and took the town's supply of food, its silver, and some of the richest Creoles into the granary, which, being built of stone on the slope of a steep hill, was all but impregnable. Its only vulnerable spot was its single wooden door. Hidalgo's forces might have stormed it forever to no avail. But a wizened little miner of the area, his lungs already ruined by mine-dust, volunteered to break the door down. He protected his back with a flagstone, climbed the hill amid the Spaniards' bullets, fired the door with dynamite, and let in the besieging forces. The Spanish commandant within was killed by a single stone from an Indian's slingshot.

Then, his army grown to eighty thousand, Hidalgo pressed on into the towering, pine-covered mountains between Toluca and the valley of Mexico, where, ten thousand feet high, he fought a battle with the main body of the viceroy's army and defeated them.

But at that point, with Mexico City spread out in full view in the valley below them, Hidalgo unaccountably withdrew, and the rebels lost the initiative. From then on, it was disaster.

He attempted to recapture his momentum, and faced the Spanish army once more on the plains northwest of Guadalajara. But a munitions wagon exploded, the dry grass caught fire, and a brushfire routed the rebel army, taking a terrible toll. The aging priest, retreating northward through the deserts of Chichuahua, was betrayed, ambushed, and captured.

He was tried by the Inquisition, that terrifying arm of the Roman Catholic church. After four months' imprisonment, he was brought out to face the firing squad. The soldiers who had to shoot the old priest trembled so they could hardly aim, and it took several volleys before they were finally able to kill him. His head and those of Allende and two other rebel leaders were hung in cages from the four corners of the granary on the hill he had stormed near Guanajuato. The church which Hidalgo had served his whole life and which had already excommunicated him and executed him, now ordered every portrait of him, every letter he had ever written, destroyed. It wished to wipe out every shred of evidence that he had ever existed.

The cause of liberty was not lost, however. Another priest, who had been sent by Hidalgo toward the south with twenty-five men, had increased his forces, and for four years went on to fight doggedly and brilliantly through the mountains and valleys and coastal jungles of the areas we now know as Guerrero, Veracruz, Michoacán, Morelos, Oaxaca. This was José María Morelos, a plump, swarthy mestizo scarcely five feet tall, who had worked as a peon on an hacienda and almost starved to death putting himself through a religious seminary.

Father Morelos proved to have the military genius and the political foresight that his predecessor lacked. In the hot, sleepy little town of Chilpancingo, he and some of his fellow rebels drew up a tentative constitution. It was designed to create a republic, guarantee racial equality, and bind all men to the same law (under Spanish rule, the churchmen and the army were exempt from civil law). It also decreed that the vast holdings of the church and the great haciendas were to be broken up and distributed to the peasants. When Morelos was captured in 1815, this document was enough to condemn him. Like

Father Hidalgo before him, he was adjudged guilty by the Inquisition and put to death.

The Mexicans were not the only Latin Americans pitted against Spain in this fateful decade. Since 1810, Creoles in South America like Simón Bolívar and José San Martín had also been leading their countrymen in a valiant fight for freedom, taking their armies on incredible marches over the almost impassable Andes Mountains to challenge the Spanish forces. Bit by bit, Spain's leadership in the New World was crumbling.

By 1817, however, the revolution in Mexico seemed all but destroyed. The guerrilla leaders who had fought for Morelos had been captured, shot, or subdued. A few, like the former law student Guadalupe Victoria, had disappeared into the jungle to live to fight another day.

But some of their ideas had begun to take root. Within a few years even the most conservative Mexicans had come to believe the country should govern itself. It was thanks to a most unlikely alliance between the conservatives and a few of the surviving rebel leaders that independence was finally achieved.

In 1821, the year that fifteen-year-old Benito Juárez ended his solitary studies by rosin-light and entered the seminary in Oaxaca, the inhabitants of Mexico's capital some three hundred miles to the north witnessed a curious ceremony. Brilliantly uniformed and riding a black horse at the head of his army, a vainglorious former

Spanish general named Agustín de Iturbide made a triumphal entry into the colonial capital and was handed the keys of the city by the rebellious city fathers. Along with several former rebel leaders, he declared Mexico's freedom from Spain. At long last!

But this declaration came to be known as the "False Independence," because within a short time Iturbide turned on his allies and, in a pitiful attempt to emulate Napoleon Bonaparte, announced himself Emperor of Mexico.

The Mexicans were outraged, and Iturbide was soon forced to flee, leaving behind him a congress which was struggling to write a constitution for the new nation. Now, perhaps, the problems of the unenfranchised, uneducated, landless Indians who made up 80 per cent of the country would be dealt with.

The answer came two years later. Guadalupe Victoria, the rebel leader who had evaded capture by living thirty months in the Veracruz jungles subsisting on nuts and fruits, became Mexico's first president. But the constitution which Congress presented by no means met the needs of the Mexican people. Although it was supposedly patterned on the Constitution of the United States, there were tragic omissions in it. Juárez, looking back on it years afterward, said that it laid the groundwork for all the miseries and upheavals his country was to suffer for generations. There was no guarantee of trial by jury, for instance. The church and the army were still laws unto themselves and exempt from civil law. The vast holdings of the church could not be taxed. And Catholicism was the only religion to be allowed.

But here and there, in various corners of the young republic, a few liberals struggled on, trying to create a better life for the millions of Indians who were still landless and still disfranchised. They labored to break the church's stranglehold on education, and in Oaxaca, they succeeded. In 1827, the Institute of Sciences and Arts, a civil college, opened its doors. And though the church stormed, and called its faculty and students "heretics" and "libertines," the school survived. A year after its founding, twenty-two-year-old Benito Juárez enrolled and began the study of law.

4

INFLUENCES

Oaxaca
1828-1834

The gentle old bookbinder may have had his regrets that Benito had not chosen a religious life. He may also have been troubled by the church's attack on the new institution, but the attack was clearly unfounded. After all, the school's first director was a Dominican father, and several of its staff were priests. So once again, he had acceded to the young man's wishes. Benito left his godfather's home for the last time, to enter the challenging and exciting life of the new school.

How different it was from the stale, dead atmosphere of the seminary! Here, in addition to law, one could study mathematics and logic, physics, medicine, French, English, and government. At times the teachers stepped aside and let the students lead classroom discussions. The many political problems of the day were thrashed out, prejudices were ventilated and discarded, new opinions and ideals came into being. Some young men shrank from this painful exposure to fresh ideas, or were intimidated by the church's bitter campaign against the Institute, and retreated to the quiet safety of the seminary. But Benito Juárez remained.

He studied. He learned. His teacher of logic, Miguel Mendez, was a fiery young idealist just a year older than Juárez, and, like himself, an Indian who had come down from the sierra and gone through the seminary. Mendez was tubercular, but this did not dampen his ardor or silence his passionate discussions. When classes were over, students would gather in his room to continue their arguments on the day's issues. One day Mendez pointed out Juárez to the others, and said, "This one here, who's so serious and reserved—he will be a great politician. He will rise higher than any of us, and he will be one of our great men and the glory of our country!"

That year and the next, the newborn country was going through the throes of a presidential election, and already its democratic processes were breaking down. A former guerrilla leader, Vicente Guerrero, had run for president, but the army had rigged the elections in many of the states and defeated him. Guerrero's followers rebelled in protest, and the governor of Veracruz, Antonio López de Santa Anna, had joined the rebellion and come storming into Oaxaca to lay siege to the local monastery. The surprised Oaxacans had offered no resistance. In fact, when the nation's Congress hastily proclaimed

Guerreo president the following year, the Institute gave Santa Anna a dinner of celebration.

The night of the banquet, Benito Juárez was waiting on table at the Institute. It was his regular work and paid for his education. As he went quietly about his task barefoot, in the white cotton trousers and smock traditionally worn by his people, the ambitious Santa Anna gave him no more than a glance. Why should he? There was nothing about the stolid, reserved young Indian, short of stature, wide-cheekboned and dark of skin, to make anyone take a second look.

But in later years Santa Anna would remember the encounter with bitterness.

Actually, the Zapotecs were known as a people of great dignity, with a profound sense of their own rights and the rights of others, and with a tradition of local self-government that dated back hundreds of years before the Conquest. One of the Spanish conquistadors had said, "If there is any justice to be found anywhere, it is among these people."

And history was moving rapidly. Mexico needed men who could look at her problems dispassionately and think ahead to a different sort of future. Juárez had no family, no ties to the colonial past, and no habits of conventional, upper-middle-class thought and behavior. He could face the idea of change with clear eyes.

There was personal grief in store for him in 1830. His teacher and mentor, the young Zapotec Miguel Mendez, died of typhus. But his ideas did not die. Many of them had taken root and flourished in Benito's mind.

Slowly, Juárez was moving ahead, studying and showing a surprising range of ability outside his chosen field of law. In 1831 he was appointed substitute for the professor of physics at the Institute, an assignment which also augmented his meager income. Later that year, he reached a goal he had been moving toward ever since he'd begun his studies there. He began an apprenticeship in a lawyer's office in Oaxaca. And he took still another step forward. He was elected an alderman of the city.

It was a slow and steady pace. But ahead. Always ahead.

Meanwhile, the exciting and dramatic figures of Mexico's political life appeared like rockets against the sky, inflaming the popular imagination, and then, as often as not, perishing, suddenly, as rockets do. After months of disorder in the country, Vicente Guerrero, who had set a pattern for rebellion which was to persist tragically for many decades, was himself forced to flee. After a period of resistance, he was lured aboard a boat in Acapulco harbor, and the captain sold him to the Mexican government for fifty thousand pesos. He was brought to Oaxaca and tried. But now his former ally Santa Anna would have nothing to do with him, and at last, condemned, he was taken to the tropical province west of Oaxaca and executed. His vice-president, Anastasio Bustamante, who had led the revolt against him, became president and then dictator. And then he too was overthrown.

Poor Mexico! She had been plundered by the Spaniards for three centuries, left still poorer by a dozen years of revolution, and had no history of self-government to help her find her way. It was small wonder that she was going through tumultuous days. The church and the army were, of course, still exempt from civil law. And the various state governments, empowered by the new constitution to manage national elections in their own manner, were easily manipulated or overthrown. The result, during those few years, was that liberal governments of eleven states were overthrown, liberal politicians jailed or shot, and newspapers ruthlessly suppressed.

Little of this turmoil was reflected in Oaxaca, however. Its quiet streets were not disturbed by the disorders that rent the capital. Its clear high air echoed, as always, with the sound of bells from its innumerable churches, and from the green-brown hills, the mounds of Monte Alban looked down serenely over the valley and the city. Juárez went on preparing himself for the bar examination, and was by now a full professor of physics at the Institute. He was elected *diputado*, deputy, to the state's legislature, and by now he had discarded the Indian smock for a respectable black suit.

For one brief year (April 1833–April 1834), it was a good time to be a liberal. In Mexico City, Santa Anna had led a brief revolt against the government and had been proclaimed president. He appointed two highly respected liberal philosophers, Luis Moya and Valentín Gómez Farias, to function in his stead, and then withdrew to his country estate pleading illness. But he must have had some deeper reason for such uncharacteristic reticence.

Moya and Farias immediately astounded the nation by introducing a series of reforms. They stripped the army of its *fueros* (extralegal privileges), and declared that henceforth soldiers and officers were to be tried in civil, not military, courts, and must abide by civil law. They placed the church under the same order, and declared that Mexican citizens were no longer under obligation to pay whatever tribute their local parish priest demanded of them. The University of Mexico, in the capital, was removed from church control, and a few public schools were established, independent of the church.

The army, the church, and many of Mexico's wealthy and conservative citizens would have resisted these encroachments on their special privileges in any event, but something else happened that year to further undermine the new program. There was a cholera epidemic.

It had swept Paris the year before, and now it reached Mexico, decimating the people of the capital. In Oaxaca, the sunny pastels of the colonial houses paled as black-and-yellow flags, the sign of the plague, were posted everywhere. The commonest sights on the street were funeral corteges, dead-carts trundling over the cobbles with their burdens, and groups of grieving Indians, in black, accompanying their coffins on foot to the cemetery. All over Mexico churchmen cried out that the dread disease was God's visitation on the country in punishment for the new laws.

Santa Anna waited until the people were weakened, frightened, and exhausted, and the army and clergy in almost open revolt, then swept back into the capital to send the two liberals, Moya and Farias, packing, and their new laws with them. The army's and church's special privileges were restored. Santa Anna disbanded the states' governing bodies and set himself up as absolute dictator. The "Age of Santa Anna" had begun.

During the war for independence, this wealthy Creole had helped the Spaniards hound down Father Hidalgo. But when it looked as though rebellion was a winning cause, he joined it. He bred fighting cocks, and on his various military adventures transported his ferocious birds with him. In the state of Veracruz he owned an enormous estate known as Manga de Clavo. It spread over miles of tropical jungle filled with every kind of exotic bird and flower, and here and there his peons' thatched huts were visible amid the trees, primitive as those of prehistoric man.

Santa Anna at this time was about forty, of middle height, black-eyed, black-haired, with heavy features and an air of sorrowful elegance about him that deceived almost everyone—at first. Now, having waited on the sidelines until he felt the liberals were thoroughly discredited, he had returned to the capital as "Mexico's savior." He would play this role four separate times, to be violently deposed just as often. And he would recur in Juárez's life from time to time like an evil genius.

With his reappearance, and with the tide of liberalism reversed all over the country, the administration of Oaxaca fell. In the town of Tehuacán, Juárez was peremptorily arrested and confined within the limits of the city for the "crime" of having belonged to a political party now in disfavor with the president.

He was released just as summarily, and returned to practicing law in Oaxaca. But by now it was not Santa Anna who was uppermost in his mind. There was another figure looming large on the young Zapotec's horizon, a man who would confirm Juárez's convictions in a cause that would occupy him for most of his life.

The church was still almost omnipotent in Mexico, as it had been all during Spanish rule. Years later, Juárez would look back on this period and write that the people were forced to pay tributes to the church "in accordance with the will and greed of the curates." There were, he said, some honorable and upright pastors, who levied only moderate charges on their flocks, but such men were rare. For the most part, "the citizens groaned in their oppression and misery. . . . Justice, if they sought it, was usually deaf to them, and often they received in answer scorn and imprisonment.

"I myself," he went on, "have been both a witness and a victim of one of these injustices."

In the village of Loricha, not too far from the city of Oaxaca, the parish priest had made life miserable for his parishioners, demanding payments and personal services out of all proportion to those customarily rendered. In 1834, a group of villagers had come to the state's capital and sought out the man they thought most likely to help them defend themselves against the priest. He was Benito Juárez, many of whose clients were either poor, or Indian, or both.

Juárez listened to their complaints. It was not an unfamiliar story. He took the case and obtained a temporary judgment against the priest. But almost immediately the man was back in Loricha again, exercising his influence over the local officials. Juárez received word that the villagers who had complained had been arrested and thrown in jail, where they were being held incommunicado. More than that, there was an order out that if anyone else from Loricha tried to contact Juárez, or obtain legal help from any other lawyer, they too would be arrested and imprisoned.

Juárez had much to occupy him. He not only had his practice to attend to, but by that time was a teacher of law at his beloved Institute. He was, however, so aroused at the flagrant injustice to his clients that he obtained a leave of absence from his teaching and went to the village of Miahuatlán, where they were being held.

The local judge greeted him politely enough, and Juárez asked him what the charge against his prisoners was.

Unfortunately, said the judge, he couldn't give out that information. The case was being kept secret. Juárez insisted that the judge read him the arrest warrant, which by law must be made public.

The judge parried. Juárez must come back next day, with a properly drawn-up petition.

But when Juárez returned the next day, the judge's respectful attitude had vanished. He spoke angrily to him and imposed all sorts of outrageous legal demands. When Juárez protested, the judge ordered him to be silent and to reappear that afternoon to answer to a charge of vagrancy.

Juárez realized that the priest and the judge between them might go to even greater lengths. He made his way back to Oaxaca to lodge a complaint, only to find that here too the priest had done his work. Juárez could make no headway whatsoever in the matter of the unhappy prisoners.

Even that was not enough for the vengeful curate.

At midnight one night soon after, the judge of the Court of Justice in Oaxaca knocked on Juárez's door and personally escorted him to jail. He told him only that he was to be sent as a prisoner to Miahuatlán for fomenting rebellion and disorder in the village of Loricha, a place where Juárez had never set foot in in his life!

It was nine days before Juárez could get release on bail, and the Superior Court refused to take any action whatsoever against either the judge of Miahuatlán or the priest of Loricha.

If such injustice could fall upon Juárez, with all his knowledge of the law and his reputation for probity in Oaxaca, what justice could be expected for the helpless and unprotected? Daily, he saw fresh evidence of the misery in store for those unhappy souls who had incurred the wrath of the wealthy, or the military, or the clergy. Decades later he would write in his memoirs for his children, that he had been *confirmed in my determination to work constantly for the destruction of the evil power of the privileged classes.* And that *society could never be happy while those classes existed hand-in-glove with the public powers.*

5

SEEDS OF A WAR TO COME

Oaxaca
1835-1846

The curate of Loricha had shown the way. But Juárez moved slowly, and during the eight or nine years following his own private conflict with the church, he left few indelible marks of his existence on the public records of Oaxaca. He was still unmarried. He was not growing rich, because so much of his law practice was among the poor. However, when he was thirty-five years old, he was named Judge of Prosecution for the state's capital, and in the two years that followed, served honorably.

But if Juárez knew what *his* direction was, his troubled country did not. With violent swings of the pendulum, conservative government followed liberal, and back again, usually as a result of a military uprising. One Mexican historian has estimated that there was a revolution every time Mexico's national debt reached over 25 per cent. When the government's treasury was empty, it could not pay its generals, soldiers, or civil servants, and at this point they would support almost any rebellious candidate who promised them their back wages. Since the country's expenditures were often almost double its income, revolts were frequent.

The lack of strength and continuity in Mexico's government allowed a dangerous situation to develop in the north, one which would cost the country almost half its territory. And the man who would play the strongest role, as both hero and villain, was Santa Anna.

For a decade following the defeat of the Spaniards, American colonists had been settling on the rich farm and grazing land of Mexico's Texas territory. By agreement with the young republic, they were to assume all the responsibilities of Mexican citizenship, in exchange for the right to purchase their acreage cheaply. By the early 1830s there were between twenty and thirty thousand of these settlers, as well as a large number of Negro slaves brought down to work in the cotton fields. This was in open violation of Mexico's law forbidding slavery.

Before long both sides were unhappy with the arrangement. More colonists were pouring in, and Mexicans regarded such a large body of undigested foreigners much as the proverbial Arab regarded the camel with one foot in the tent. They feared they might soon take over the whole tent.

The colonists, for their part, had come to think of Texas as their own. They chafed at Mexico's lack of trial by jury. There were no licensed seaports nearby from which they could ship their produce abroad. And Mexico insisted on collecting duties along the Louisiana border, which was, at that time, the border between the two countries. By early 1836, the settlers were close to open rebellion.

Santa Anna, then the dictator of Mexico, mortgaged his estate Manga de Clavo to equip an army, and marched it across the burning deserts to Coahuila to quell the rebellious colonists.

A tiny group of 150 Texan soldiers prepared to defend themselves in an old mission in San Antonio called the Alamo. After two weeks of siege, Santa Anna's trumpets sounded the call, "No quarter!" His soldiers stormed the mission and killed every man inside.

But elsewhere in the territory, Texan independence had already been declared. Big, hard-drinking Sam Houston, who had once been a chief among the Cherokee Indians, took his army of seven or eight hundred Texans toward the San Jacinto River, where, in April, the two armies confronted each other. Houston attacked, and amazingly, caught Santa Anna's men cooking their dinner. With shouts of "Remember the Alamo!" the Texans defeated the Mexicans and killed six hundred of them, taking the rest prisoner. Santa Anna fled. He was found next day in his carpet slippers, hiding in the tall grass.

The battles solved nothing. Santa Anna offered to

barter Texas's independence for his own freedom, but the rest of Mexico thought it a poor exchange and refused to second the offer. They would not recognize Texan independence, but neither, during the nine years that followed, did they take steps to reconquer the area.

And the United States, already embroiled in dissension between slave and free states, could not admit another slave-holding state into the Union at this moment in its history. So Texas existed for a time as an independent republic in the eyes of the United States, as a rebellious territory in the eyes of Mexico, and as the focus of countless raids and skirmishes between small groups of Texans and Mexicans, which bred deep hostility on both sides.

Santa Anna returned from captivity to find that his proposed bargain had cost him his popularity, and beat a tactical retreat to his hacienda. In 1838, however, Mexico became involved in a brief, comic-opera war with France, during which Santa Anna and his men did battle against a French squadron at Veracruz. The French won the day, but one of their cannonballs took off Santa Anna's leg, which made him a hero again. The leg was buried with full military honors at Manga de Clavo.

In 1841 he returned to Mexico City to overthrow the government once more. With the help of the clergy he again installed himself as president-dictator. His leg was dug up and brought to the cathedral in the nation's capital for reburial, with greater solemnity than before.

Economic troubles continued to plague the country. The generals' wages were overdue, and an uprising threw Santa Anna out of office once again. He fled. The populace in the capital were furious with him by that time, and a crowd dug up his leg and trailed it through the streets on the end of a string. The irrepressible revolutionary was captured and exiled to Cuba for ten years. Even in exile, however, plotting was a chronic condition with him. In 1845 he outdid himself in treachery, precipitating the bitterest event in Mexico's history to that moment.

In Oaxaca, a major change had taken place in Juárez's life. In his memoirs he wrote simply, "On July 31, 1843, I married doña Margarita Maza, daughter of don Antonio Maza and of doña Petra Parada." The Mazas were the family to whom twelve-year-old Benito had gone after his all-day descent from the mountain, and it was in their household that his sister worked as a cook. They had taken him in and sheltered him then, and now they accepted him as a son-in-law.

Margarita had not even been born when the runaway had come to the Mazas. When she married Juárez she was seventeen and he thirty-seven. Of her bridegroom, the young bride had written, "He is very homely—but very good."

Nowhere in Juárez's memoirs did he deal with his own problems or his own emotions. There is no way of knowing whether the Mazas raised objections over the marriage of their gently bred daughter to this man whose origins were so humble. Perhaps they, like Margarita, saw that he was "very good." Perhaps, like Margarita, they saw the wise and steady man within the stolid Indian exterior.

In any event, Margarita would prove as worthy of her husband as he of her. She would bear him twelve children, and in time of trouble would sacrifice all she owned to help him. She would follow him through physical hardships that were almost impossible to contemplate. Juárez called her his *viejecita*, his "little old woman," and they loved each other till the day of her death.

During the next few years Juárez proceeded slowly, steadily, meeting almost daily proof that "politics is the art of the possible." He became a member of the governor's cabinet and worked to promote small, but important, improvements: a road from Oaxaca to Tehuacán, court reforms, a new sanitary commission. The current governor was a Santa Anna man, and Juárez made small concessions to him, but never big ones. He would assist at an unveiling of a portrait of Santa Anna, for instance, but when the army drafted a student for criticizing the governor, Juárez resigned his office immediately.

Oaxacans were coming to know and respect him. He was unanimously elected to the state legislature, and then was appointed president of Oaxaca's supreme court. At last, in 1846, when foreign troops were already on Mexico's soil, a national election was held, and Benito Juárez was sent as a delegate from Oaxaca to the nation's congress in Mexico City.

6

A BRIEF AND BITTER HARVEST

Mexico City
1846-1847

Popocatepetl and Ixtaccihuatl looked down over the valley of Mexico. The valley itself was seven thousand feet high, and the now extinct volcanoes towered so far above that their peaks were crowned perpetually in snow. Popo's single, clean sweep of cone was beautiful to see. It was no wonder the Aztecs had worshipped it as a god, and given it as consort the sprawling, several-summited "white sleeping lady" beyond.

Below, in the valley, the Aztecs had long ago built their city Tenochtitlán on an island in the midst of a great lake. Over the centuries the lake had receded from its banks, but flooded now and then in the rainy season. The great pyramids of the pre-Columbian city had been razed by the Spaniards and replaced by a cathedral, built stone by stone by the captive Indians. The city's central plaza, the zócalo, was tree-lined now, the cathedral forming one side of the square and the National Palace another. Along the street of San Francisco, the most beautiful of the capital, stood elegant colonial buildings, one built altogether of blue tile which glistened in the sun. And close by was the tree-lined park, the Alameda.

Here and there about the city were long stretches of the ancient aqueducts, supported on arches of stone, which the Aztecs and later the Spaniards had built to carry water from the springs of Chapultepec Park to the city's heart. If one followed them west from the center of town, one reached the incredible greenery of Chapultepec itself, the Aztecs' "hill of grasshoppers," where their emperor Moctezuma had once had his palace. The Spaniards had built their own castle there, its battlements topping a sudden outcropping of rock in the midst of the great cypresses and elms and Indian laurels of the park. The castle had recently become the military college, where young cadets were trained to become soldiers for the young nation.

When the novice *diputado* arrived from Oaxaca late in the winter of 1846, he was met by all too much evidence of the tragic distance between Mexico's rich and Mexico's poor. Elegant carriages, some of them costing as much as ten thousand dollars, rumbled over the cobbled streets with their beautifully dressed passengers. Along the sidewalks swarmed the tragically poor, the Indian mothers cradling their babies in *rebozos*, the cripples flaunting their deformities to beg for centavos. And, their wares spread out for display, sellers of tortillas hovered over little mounds of lard, of a dozen kinds of chiles, of woven mats and plaster-of-Paris religious figures and fragile wooden toys. There were soot-covered charcoal sellers. There were men with bamboo cages of birds strapped to their foreheads and others carrying yokes with deep ewers of milk. And all, as they shouted their wares, were inadequately clad for the cold December air of this high altitude, and few had had enough to eat.

Congress opened the first of December. For Juárez, it was not a time to make speeches or to distinguish himself. It was enough for him to sit silently, to listen and to vote, and above all, to learn.

The new year began. For Mexico, this year of 1847 was to be the bitterest year since it became a republic, and the most humiliating.

To the north, there were many American politicians who espoused the cause of "Manifest Destiny." These men, some of whom were in President Polk's cabinet, felt that it was the duty of the United States to spread its agricultural and industrial superiority all the way to the shores of the Pacific, and southward across Mexico to the isthmus of Tehuantepec. Mexico's anxiety about Texas, therefore, was understandable. And when, in 1845, the United States voted to annex the Texas territory, Mexico girded to defend herself.

During negotiations between the two countries, Santa Anna, still in exile in Havana, was not idle. According to accounts published later, he secretly sent an emissary to Washington to suggest that the States purchase the disputed territory. However, he pointed out, no Mexican president could accept such an offer and survive in office. Instead, the United States must go through the motions of putting military and naval pressure on Mexico to support its offer. If he were in office, he indicated, he would settle the matter to their liking!

Whether or not this proposal had any effect on United States policy, by March of 1846 General Zachary Taylor had moved his troops southward to the Rio Grande River. The Mexican settlers had resisted, and President Polk had declared that Mexico had shed American blood on American soil and that a state of war existed between the two countries. General Taylor ("Old Rough and Ready") had taken a number of towns in northern Mexico. A naval squadron blockaded Veracruz, and American warships had turned up at San Francisco to capture California, which, Mexicans suspected, they had wanted all along.

Not all Americans approved of these actions. A Whig congressman from Kentucky declared, "It is our own President who began this war." A young Army lieutenant named Ulysses S. Grant wrote later in his memoirs, "I do not think there was ever a more wicked war than that waged by the United States on Mexico. I thought so too at the time, when I was but a youngster, only I had not moral courage enough to resign."

And a young congressman from Illinois named Abraham Lincoln jeopardized his political future by stating publicly that the first blood of the war was shed not on American but on Mexican soil. "It is a fact that the United States Army in marching to the Rio Grande marched into a peaceful Mexican settlement, and frightened the inhabitants away from their homes and growing crops." He was convinced, he wrote, that President Polk was *"deeply conscious of being in the wrong* [italics author's]."

But Manifest Destiny prevailed. American forces were by now deep in Mexico, and that invasion, and defeat, would create an anger and resentment that Mexicans would still be nursing more than a century later.

Meanwhile, the ambitious Santa Anna was back in Mexico. As the only leader powerful enough to command the country at this time, he had been invited back by the liberal Dr. Gómez Farias; and in order to be allowed past the American blockade at Veracruz, he had made enticing promises to the enemy.

Now he was leading his army in unsuccessful stands against the Americans throughout the north of Mexico. Everywhere, there was disaster for the Mexican forces. They lost the seaport of Tampico, and the ancient island fortress of San Juan de Ulúa in Veracruz harbor. Near Saltillo, at a place known as La Angostura, Santa Anna with a superior force came so close to victory—only to withdraw—that many Mexicans were convinced he had lost the battle deliberately.

Who knows? Perhaps it was true, and Santa Anna was

merely repaying the Americans for past favors. Or perhaps he reasoned that his convenient military "defeats"
would ensure United States support of his future political
career. In whichever case, treachery at home gave him
the chance to appear once more as Mexico's "strong
man."

In an attempt to finance the country's defense, Dr.
Gómez Farias had declared a tax on church property.
The clergy was furious, and with their collaboration, an
army regiment known as the "Polkos" mutinied in the
capital. The Polkos were so called because they were
dandies, devoted to ballroom dancing and, apparently, to
the special privileges of the church. Their wartime mutiny in Mexico City did indeed seem to prove that a tax
on church property was to them more serious than an
American victory over Mexico.

Fresh from his defeat at La Angostura, Santa Anna
rushed back to the capital, turned his coat once more and
declared with the Polkos, threw out Gómez Farias, and
again exempted church property from taxation. This at a
time when the church controlled between one third and
one half of the wealth of the country.

He also withheld payment of salaries to the liberal
deputies of Congress, including Benito Juárez.

Juárez knew that on a national level there was little
one lone, and unpaid, deputy could do to help his tor-
mented country. He had also learned that the legislature
of Oaxaca had been overturned by those who supported

the Polkos. In Oaxaca, at least, his efforts might be of help in restoring the state's government.

He went home.

Meanwhile, the Mexican army was facing its Calvary. Cut to pieces in a battle at Cerro Gordo, they were now reassembling to face the enemy in the valley of Mexico. The torrential summer rains came on. In August, the bells of the cathedral on the zócalo rang out their portentous warning that the American army had penetrated into the valley.

All during the month of August the Mexican army met the enemy, on lakeside and hillside and on the edge of the huge lava bed south of the city; at Chalco, and Contreras, and Churubusco. No one had thought the motley group of Indians, mestizos, and Creoles capable of such courage, but they were now prepared to die in defense of their city. When the American army drew near Chapultepec Park, a group of young cadets, some only fourteen and fifteen years old, wrapped themselves in the Mexican flag and jumped from the battlements to their deaths on the rocks below rather than lose the flag to the invaders.

Even that pathetic sacrifice was in vain. On September 14, 1847, General Winfield Scott and his men marched into the zócalo, and the war was over.

7

"MYSELF A SON OF THE PEOPLE"

Oaxaca
1847-1853

The day before the fall of Mexico City, Santa Anna had fled. In the weeks that followed, he made his way south, eventually reaching the border of Oaxaca. There he was turned back, by order of Oaxaca's newly appointed provisional governor.

The governor was Benito Juárez.

Angry and embittered, Santa Anna continued his flight, to his home state of Veracruz and from there to exile once more, in Jamaica. But he would not forget the humiliation he had suffered, and, being a man who always put personalities ahead of principles, could only interpret Juárez's order in light of his own temperament. Years later he wrote bitterly of the incident: "He [Juárez] could not forgive me because he had waited on me at table in Oaxaca, in December 1829, with his bare feet on the floor and in his linen smock and trousers. . . . It is amazing that an Indian of such low degree should have figured in Mexico as he has. . . ."

During that fateful August, Juárez had reached his home state, and had helped his friends overturn the rebellious Polkos and reestablish the state legislature. By November he was appointed provisional governor, and swore in his oath of office to defend the laws of Oaxaca and "the Catholic, Apostolic, and Roman religion, without permitting any other in the state." This he could do in good conscience, because although he was not blind to its excesses, he was still a faithful member of the church.

His inaugural address mentioned those of his compatriots whom he thought more worthy of being governor. Perhaps, he said, he should have refused this post. But "today, when the fountains of the public treasury are drained and the sources of obedience and morality are exhausted as a result of internal dissensions; today, finally, when the unjust invader occupies the capital of the republic and threatens us with the total conquest of our territory, the first magistracy of the state is no more than an outpost of imminent danger and a heavy load that will produce nothing but anxieties, fatigues, and sufferings." Therefore, he told his fellow Oaxacans, he was there to serve.

He stood before them in his black frock coat, a modest, almost humble man, with his dark Indian face and short, stocky body, looking like anything in the world but the governor of a state, and promised the Oaxacans that his first duty would be to the law and the needs of the people. But there was something more. "Free, and for me sacred," he said, "is the *right to think; and my compatriots will not be molested for their opinions revealed in speech or writing* [italics author's]." He promised prosecution of those who violated the rights of others. And he reminded his constituents of the anguish of their homeland. "If we draw upon our uttermost strength, still there may be time for us to save her. But if . . . it should be decided that she should vanish from the list of free nations, let us work so that on perishing beneath her ruins, we shall leave to posterity records that will honor our memory."

Among the crowd that had come to see Juárez's inauguration was a group of his fellow villagers who had walked the long distance down the mountain from Guelatao. They had brought him gifts of hens, fruits, vegetables, and grains. Afterward, the little group in their sandals and white *calzones* and smocks made their way to his side, and the spokesman addressed him in awkward, formal terms:

"We come to see you, Benito, in the name of your village, to tell you that we are happy that you are Governor. You know our needs, and you will help us, because you are good and will not forget that you are one of us."

Juárez knew what a sacrifice the gifts of fowl and produce meant to an impoverished people. He gave them a peso, as a token that he would do what he could for them, and invited them to spend the night in the municipal palace, the same palace where his father had dropped dead peddling fruit almost forty years before.

His first act in fulfillment of his pledge to the people of Guelatao was to build them a school.

Two years later he was elected governor again, and in his second inaugural address he spoke even more directly to his fellow Indians. "Myself a son of the people," he said, "I shall not forget them. On the contrary, I shall provide for their education, and see that they grow and make a future for themselves. . . ."

And during his regime he did establish schools, several hundred of them, for both women and men. Among them were also eight normal schools for the training of much-needed teachers. But he knew enough about his land and its people to realize another truth: that lack of education was not the primary evil afflicting Mexico. There was a more serious problem: poverty. "The man who lacks the wherewithal to feed his family," he said, "considers the education of his children a remote benefit. . . . Relieve him of the fetters which poverty and despotism impose on him, and he will awaken naturally. . . ."

To combat poverty roads had to be built so that his people could get their produce to market. Oaxacans needed a port on the Pacific from which handicrafts and foodstuffs could be shipped. They needed honest government so that their tax money would not go to line the pockets of dishonest bureaucrats, and they needed peace from the incessant civil strife. And, of course, schools. It would be no small task, particularly since, at the beginning of Juárez's regime, the treasury of Oaxaca was empty and the state more than a hundred thousand dollars in debt.

The governor's mansion, to which Juárez and Margarita and their children moved, was a big, rather ugly building in the middle of the city, only two or three blocks from the State House. There were bustling street noises outside, and bells from the nearby cathedral made the walls resound. But Juárez was used to humble quarters, and this new dwelling was more than ample to house his ever-increasing family. Too, all its rooms looked out on a big, airy central patio, verdant with plants and flowers.

He and Margarita oversaw the older children's education and music lessons. When they could, they attended the theater or concerts, but the spectacle of the bullfight, the trumpets and the excitement, did not appeal to Juárez. He did not think a man should risk his life for the entertainment of the multitude.

The Oaxacans soon learned there was another area in which don Benito differed from his predecessors—promptitude.

The Spanish Catholics had never had the Anglo-Saxon, Protestant admiration for toil as a virtue, and for the Indians, during three hundred years of colonialism, work had been synonymous with slavery. Thus, traditionally, regular working hours meant little to the people of the new republic. Local officials drifted in and out of office when it pleased them, and vanished at midday for three-hour dinners. Oaxacans were astonished, therefore, when their new governor appeared in his black frock coat every morning at the State House at exactly nine o'clock. "Like a common brick-layer!" one of them complained. Not only that, he expected all government employees to do likewise. And henceforth they would be allowed an hour, no more, for *comida*, the midday meal.

Worse, those civil servants who had got their jobs through relatives or influential friends found themselves fired, and their places filled by men of known competence, regardless of their political affiliations. This meant, of course, that Juárez's program received the support of men of every shade of political opinion.

Whatever Juárez's inner convictions about the privileges of the clergy, however, this was not the time to risk a confrontation. He may have disapproved of the use of civil force to collect payment of tithes to the church, but it was the law, and he enforced it. In return, when he wanted a road built to the Pacific port of Huatluco (now called Puerto Ángel), the local parish priests recruited volunteers to help.

All Oaxaca, rich and poor alike, cooperated in the building of the road. The priests' volunteers worked side by side with young men who were doing peon labor in exchange for exemption from the draft. Materials had been contributed by wealthy Oaxacans. Everyone did what he could, in the common endeavor.

Other roads too were built during Juárez's governorship, as well as a toll bridge over the Atoyac River which lasted a hundred years. Maps were drawn of the state, pensions established for soldiers' widows and orphans, the National Guard reorganized, and a military hospital built. For the *campesinos*, the farmers, Juárez introduced tobacco as a cash crop and taught them the principle of crop rotation. Schools sprang up in remote villages in the Sierra and elsewhere; and when in 1850 a serious outbreak of cholera occurred, he quickly established a medical commission to press a program of vaccination.

The disease took a grievous toll, however, in spite of his efforts, and of every fifty Oaxacans, one died. Among them was Juárez's two-year-old daughter, Guadalupe.

Because she was the child of the governor, he was told, she could be buried in the cathedral. But Juárez knew that such a dispensation was dangerous to public health, and as an example of obedience to the state's health laws, he himself bore the tiny coffin to the cemetery outside the walls of the city, where the city's other cholera victims were laid to rest.

These were the tragic years when Mexico was trying to recover from the effects of the American war. She had, under the terms of the Treaty of Guadalupe Hidalgo, given up Texas, California, and the largely unsettled land between, almost half her territory. She had been paid a modest cash indemnity by the Americans, but since she had borrowed heavily from foreign powers to conduct the war, her financial condition was disastrous. There were brush-fire rebellions in several states, but Oaxaca continued, as it had done all through this troublesome period, to provide soldiers, materials, and money to the federal government.

When Juárez's five years in office ended in 1852, Oaxaca's deficit was wiped out and there was a fifty-thousand-dollar surplus. It had been a gargantuan task, and he had done it with his customary self-effacing humility. To his state, he had set an example for honesty, competence, and justice which was almost unequalled in Mexico's history.

But in 1853, Santa Anna came back to power once more as president, and liberals like Juárez were marked men.

8

AMID THE ALIEN CORN

Oaxaca and New Orleans
1853-1855

In the years between 1836 and 1852, two prominent Mexican philosophers had written histories of their country, but they disagreed vigorously on both the causes and the possible cures for Mexico's problems. Actually, the men represented the two opposing schools of thought that were to rend Mexico into irreconcilable camps for generations.

An exile in Paris, aging Dr. Luis Moya had spent his final years suffering from poverty, tuberculosis, and an acute case of homesickness for his native land. Many years before, he had been part of the "false reform" of the 1820s. More recently, he had raced death to complete a work that clearly defined the liberal cause.

There were, he said, two kinds of revolution: those

like the American and British, which arose from a specific cause and reached a specific objective; and those in which "men tire of being what they are, the prevailing order irks them. . . . Everyone feels dissatisfied . . . and longs to change his condition, but no one knows precisely what he wants, and everything resolves into discontent and unrest." Such was the French Revolution, he indicated, and, by implication, Mexico's.

It was his theory that Hidalgo's revolution had miscarried, and that though the shackles of Spain had been thrown off, most of her oppressive institutions had remained, crippling all hope of true democracy for Mexico. He urged that the army, the church, and other such extralegal corporations be stripped of their privileges and become subject to civil law; that great fortunes not be allowed to accumulate indefinitely, because they tended to grow larger, to the impoverishment of the people; and that there be absolute freedom of opinion.

The opposing voice was that of a Creole aristocrat, Lucas Alamán, who deplored Mexico's war of independence altogether, and extolled the conquistador Hernando Cortés as the country's greatest benefactor. Alamán had seized leadership in 1853 following a mutiny, and promptly sent for Santa Anna to return, to unify the country and preserve the Catholic religion. He wrote the general that "we believe in the necessity of maintaining the cult in splendor, and supporting the property of the Church. . . . We are against the Federation, against the

representative system of elections. . . . We rely on the
moral force of conformity among the clergy, the landowners, and all sensible people. . . ."

Neither he nor Santa Anna voiced what was clearly
their desire—a monarchy. But on Santa Anna's return
this time there was no talk of "señor President," or even
"Your Excellency." The prodigal was now addressed as
"Most Serene Highness."

And Mexico was plunged into the most repressive period in her history. Santa Anna used the army to remove
liberal governors. He banned any newspaper which
spoke of him with less than praise, and he shot, imprisoned, or exiled his political opponents—all in the name
of preventing civil disorder.

It was the end of May, a time of heat and dryness
before the onset of the summer rains. Benito Juárez had
returned to Oaxaca's Institute of Arts and Sciences as its
director, and had resumed his law practice, many of his
clients being Indians in remote villages of the sierra.

Some of the villages could only be reached on mule-
back, along tortuous trails. It would be a deeply devoted
lawyer who would make his way into these tiny hamlets
in the mountains. Juárez had been to Ixtlán, and had
made his way back down to the little town of Etla, to
take the testimony of villagers in a case he was handling,
when the proceedings were interrupted by the arrival of a
group of armed soldiers. Señor Juárez was under arrest.

He was charged with inciting the people of the region

to class war, and was ordered to proceed, under armed guard, to Jalapa, capital of the state of Veracruz (Santa Anna's familial stronghold). He was not even allowed to bid his family good-by.

It was almost a month later that he reached the little capital city, deceptively charming with its verdure, its breathtaking vistas of white-peaked Mount Orizaba on the one hand and, spread out below to the east, the *tierra caliente*. Here he was confined for seventy-five days. On the seventy-sixth, he was arrested anew, this time by the son of Santa Anna himself, though it is doubtful whether Juárez appreciated the honor.

He was held incommunicado in an army barracks until the following day, when he was placed aboard a carriage and escorted down the steep descent into the *tierra caliente*, the hot country, below. He was driven past the coffee plantations and the tangle of jungle growth to the sun-baked city of Veracruz. From there he was taken by boat to the forbidding fortress of San Juan de Ulúa.

His cell was below water level, the walls dripped with moisture, and there were stalactites overhead. In the dark and the damp he became ill, but, as he wrote later, "I resigned myself to my fate, without uttering a complaint, without committing a humiliating act." Here he remained for twelve days, when he was summoned before the fort commander and given his passport and the order for his exile.

He was placed aboard the British packet *Avon*, but his

captors neglected to provide him with fare for his passage. Other passengers took up a collection to pay his way to the ship's first stop, Havana.

Thus, exiled and penniless, Juárez saw the shores of his native land recede from view.

Life was not much easier for Margarita, left in Oaxaca. Agents of the new governor harassed her continually, until she fled with her children to the hacienda of friends outside the city. It was difficult to get word of Juárez, or to know how he was faring. At last, she took the children to the village of Etla, where she took a small house. She sold her jewelry and opened a shop to support herself and her family. At last she heard from her husband, and realizing the terrible hardships he was under, she borrowed four hundred dollars from another *hacendado* and dispatched it to him in care of her brother, José María Maza.

Maza managed to join his brother-in-law in Havana. Juárez had heard rumors of more cholera in Oaxaca, and had been desperately worried about his family. But now, reassured, he determined to proceed to New Orleans where he knew there were other Mexicans living in exile. He and Maza got passage as sailors, and in the first days of 1854, reached the United States.

As soon as they had disembarked, they looked up their fellow exiles, and joined them in an inexpensive hotel. Before they had even lost their sea legs, they had formed a committee to consider how best to overthrow Santa Anna.

There began a period of great unhappiness for Juárez. He spent days at the quays, waiting for the arrival of boats that might bring letters from home. Such English as he had once known he had forgotten, and his companions spoke little more. Furthermore, New Orleans was in a slave state, and there was an ever-present danger that with his dark Indian skin he might be mistaken for a runaway slave.

All the Mexican exiles were dependent on such bits of money as might reach them from their friends and family at home, and at times their poverty became acute. They moved to a boardinghouse, even cheaper than the hotel, and Juárez roomed in the attic, under the eaves where in summer the heat was almost unendurable. For a time they ate lunches for ten cents apiece. Ordinarily, Juárez occupied his days studying the newspapers, constitutional law, and American colonial history. When matters became very bad indeed, he worked in a cigar factory, one of his compatriots as a waiter, and the brilliant former governor of Michoacán, Melchor Ocampo, as a potter.

Ocampo's background was as different from Juárez's as day from night. Yet such was Mexico's recent history that their experiences had run almost parallel. Ocampo was the adopted son of a wealthy Michoacán lady, whose estates he had inherited, and he had been raised with every luxury. A philosopher, naturalist, and man of letters, he had entered politics as a liberal and had served efficiently and well as his state's governor. It was during this period that, like Juárez, he too became embroiled with a local priest. In both cases their experiences dramatized for them the tyranny of the church.

The child of one of Ocampo's employees had died, and the father, being poor, asked the curate of Maravatio to bury the child free of charge. The curate refused, and when the father asked what to do with the little one's body, the curate suggested he salt it and eat it.

When Ocampo heard the story, he was outraged. He wrote a pamphlet, denouncing the power and greed of the clergy, and the battle was on. Soon he was campaigning for the right to tax church property, and against the legal right of the church to demand tithes. In April, 1853, a month before Juárez's arrest in Oaxaca, Ocampo had been arrested in Michoacán and shipped off to exile, where Juárez joined him. Ocampo was at this time forty-two years old, Juárez, forty-eight. In New Orleans the two men developed a deep respect for each other, and a friendship that lasted all their lives. Within the group of exiles, Ocampo was the activist, passionate and articulate, and Juárez was the analyst, steadfast and with a quiet patience that they all came to depend upon.

In due time, news began to reach the exiles that gave them all hope. The old Indian guerrilla, Juan Álvarez, who had fought in every one of Mexico's liberal uprisings since 1810, was organizing a rebellion in the tropical state of Guerrero, with the support of his aide Ignacio Comonfort. The rebels had met in the town of Ayutla and drawn up a plan for the overthrow of Santa Anna and a call for a constitutional convention, paralleling almost exactly the ideas of Juárez and his colleagues in New Orleans.

But at first the rebellion made little or no headway, and a few of the more faint-hearted exiles became pessimistic and went home when Santa Anna offered them what turned out to be a treacherous "amnesty." Others moved to points close to the Mexican border, where they could be within harassing distance of Santa Anna's officials on the other side. Melchor Ocampo went to Brownsville, waiting for the moment when he and his fellows could aid in an uprising in the north. All were homesick, longing for a glimpse of their homeland.

Then Juárez came down with yellow fever.

The heat in the attic room was hideous, the city foreign and unfriendly, and there was no money for medical help. Only the unremitting care of his fellow exiles kept him alive, and he did, at last, recover. He returned to work in the cigar factory. Evenings, he and his brother-in-law would take their wares to sell in saloons, and afterward, if there were any profits, they would go to the stalls of the market in the French Quarter to eat black bread and drink *café con leche*, coffee with milk. Then they would sit in the cooling evening air in one of the public squares until the sound of curfew. After curfew, no black was allowed on the city streets without written permission from his master. There was always the chance this proscription might be applied to anyone with a dark skin. So they would go home, and in the morning, if they were lucky, they might catch a fish from the Mississippi, and have enough to eat for a day or two.

At last, with uprisings against Santa Anna breaking out all over Mexico, Ignacio Comonfort wrote from Guerrero asking the exiles to join the rebellion. Ocampo and several others crossed over the border to help with the fighting in the northern states, and at the end of June, 1855, Juárez left the quays of New Orleans behind him and sailed for Acapulco.

9

THE ROAD BACK

Acapulco, Cuernavaca, Mexico City
1855

His ship touched once more at Havana, but this time, with what a difference for Juárez! Now, at last, there was reason for hope.

They traveled down the Caribbean to the Isthmus of Panama, then by rail across to the Pacific, and, again by boat, up past the sweltering ports of Central America, along Guerrero's "Costa Brava" to the bay at Acapulco. Here clustering green hills dropped suddenly down to the palm-lined shore, and the rough, storm-troubled ocean gave way to the quiet waters within the harbor.

General Juan Álvarez was at headquarters in Texca, Juárez was told, but the general's son, Colonel Diego Álvarez, was in Acapulco, and Juárez sought him out.

It was typical of Juárez that he did not identify himself. He simply stood before the colonel in the clothes he had worn throughout his exile and long voyage, and said he had come to see how he could be useful in Mexico's fight for liberty.

He didn't look as though he would make much of a soldier, hardly five feet tall and almost fifty years old. The colonel didn't know quite what to do with him. However, when he set out to join his father at headquarters, he took along the unpromising recruit.

En route, they were caught in a storm, and such shabby dignity as Juárez's clothes had possessed vanished utterly in the rain and mud. By the time they reached headquarters, he looked more like a liability than an asset to the rebel cause. Diego Álvarez managed to assemble some dry clothes for him—a pair of trooper's trousers, a blanket from Juan Álvarez's bed, and a pair of patched boots. He even managed to find a pack of cigarettes for his volunteer. But, as he wrote later, there still remained the problem of what to do with the man. "My father, who was glad to accept spontaneous collaborators in the struggle we had started against Santa Anna, was as perplexed as I; and upon his offering to serve as a secretary, and repeating that he had come to see how he could serve here where men were fighting for freedom, he was given some letters of little importance, which he answered and presented for signature with the utmost modesty."

Juárez settled into camp life, doing his modest tasks. No one questioned him further until a few days later, when a letter arrived at camp addressed to "Licenciado don Benito Juárez."

Everyone was puzzled until someone remembered the new recruit.

Still more puzzled, Diego took the letter to Juárez. "Does this mean you are a lawyer?"

"Yes, sir," said Juárez.

"Do you mean you are the same man who was governor of Oaxaca?"

"Yes, sir."

Álvarez was, in his own words, "overcome with confusion."

"But why didn't you tell me?" he asked.

"Why?" Juárez replied, shrugging his shoulders. "What difference does it make?"

In the weeks to come, however, his quiet presence would make a substantial difference.

During Juárez's period of exile in New Orleans, the reign of "His Serene Highness" Santa Anna had become more and more monarchical. He dispensed orders of nobility, and his army's uniforms and his own fairly blinded the eye with their epaulets and gold braid. The country's economy had been in disastrous condition since the war, but Santa Anna met the problem by selling the remainder of Arizona to the United States for ten million dollars, under the terms of the Gadsden Purchase.

By now, however, the general dissatisfaction manifested itself in uprisings all over the country, and the dictator, seeing the handwriting on the wall, began covertly to ship money abroad to foreign banks. He was soon in need of it. By mid-August he had abdicated and fled to South America.

His generals and former officials in Mexico City, seeing the same handwriting on the same wall, abruptly announced their approval of the rebels' "Plan of Ayutla," and appointed one of their own men temporary president of the country.

Everywhere in Mexico, rebels heard this announcement with joy without stopping to analyze its real meaning. The editor of Acapulco's newspaper asked Juárez for an article praising the action of the Mexico City generals.

But Juárez recognized the move for what it was: an attempt on the part of the generals to take over the revolution and adulterate it. He warned both Juan and Diego Álvarez, who immediately agreed with him. The following morning, as dawn was breaking over the little seaport town and fishermen were pulling in to shore with their night's catch, Juárez went to the newspaper office to make sure the editor got the facts straight before the paper went to press.

It was the same story when Mexico City's recent "converts" to the revolution sent an emissary to Álvarez's headquarters, asking the old soldier to collaborate with them in a temporary military dictatorship under a General Carrera.

Juárez sat with Álvarez at the conference table. He listened not to the words but to the meaning behind them. Then he pointed out in clear and simple terms what would become of the revolution, and what would happen to the dreams of those who had been risking their lives for a rebirth of freedom if they surrendered their leadership to Santa Anna's turncoats. He was so convincing that even the emissary was persuaded, and did not even bother to return to the capital with his report.

Álvarez's army pressed northward, out of the jungle and into the low, sun-baked rolling hills beyond. At Chilpancingo, two more emissaries arrived from Mexico City, and there was another conference. But this time, the emissaries took back with them a letter, prompted by Juárez, suggesting that since Carrera was clearly not the people's choice, he should resign.

The next word to reach the rebel army as it pushed farther north was that Carrera had done exactly that. He had stepped down from the presidency. It was now up to the various rebel leaders to put into effect their "Plan of Ayutla." Accordingly, when they reached Cuernavaca, in the lush and fertile valley of Morelos less than a day's ride from Mexico City, they halted, and in the days that followed, liberal leaders began to arrive from all over the country to meet with them and discuss the formation of a new government.

Among the other arrivals were Melchor Ocampo, Juárez's fellow exile in New Orleans, the young poet Guillermo Prieto, who would become one of Juárez's staunchest friends, and many others who had suffered and fought during Santa Anna's dictatorship. It was agreed that the presidency belonged to the man most responsible for Santa Anna's defeat, Juan Álvarez. So the weathered old Indian was sworn into office, a just reward for forty-five years of unremitting devotion to the cause of Mexican democracy.

Álvarez's first act was to appoint a cabinet: Comonfort, Melchor Ocampo, Guillermo Prieto, and Juárez. Juárez did not want any office whatsoever, but was finally persuaded to serve as minister of justice and public education.

The group went on to Mexico City, to set in motion the wheels of the new government under the temporary leadership of Comonfort. In mid-November, General Álvarez, with a body of his seasoned Indian guerrillas, rode over the mountain barrier between the valley of Morelos and the valley of Mexico, the last lap of the long, hard road from Guerrero where the battle had begun.

But once more, a cause which in the jungles and cane fields of Guerrero had been simple and heroic became muddied and obscured in the streets of the capital. Victory, in that troubled country, rarely remained victory for long.

Matters began promisingly enough. Each cabinet minister went to work in his own field, proposing legislation that would implement the cause of reform. Juárez, with his ability to see to the heart of a problem, knew that Mexico must have one set of laws for all, and one court of law for all. He proposed to General Álvarez that the separate courts of the clergy and the military be abolished. Álvarez agreed immediately, and his second-in-command, Ignacio Comonfort, carefully avoided saying either yes or no. So Juárez went to work and drafted what became known as the *Ley Juárez*, the Juárez Law.

The proposed law did away with the *fueros*, the immunities, of the clergy and the military. Henceforth, priest and bishop, soldier and officer were allowed no special privileges, but must face the same justice, in the same courts, as their fellow citizens. It was a major step in the separation of church and state, and when it was passed, late in November, the army and the clergy responded with consternation and fury. Almost immediately, minor uprisings broke out in various parts of the country.

In Mexico City too, there was beginning to be trouble. Álvarez's soldiers, many of them of Negro or Indian blood, were a new and alarming sight to the Creole residents of the capital, who liked to congratulate themselves on their fair skin. Álvarez himself, also Indian and Negro, dark-skinned, and blunt-spoken, offended the delicate sensibilities of the upper classes. They made cruel jokes about him, snubbed his public appearances, and if he went to the theater, stayed home. Juárez was bitter about this because he knew Álvarez's real worth as a man of honor and principle.

There was, however, one member of the new cabinet, Ignacio Comonfort, one of their own kind, whom the upper classes trusted. They clustered around him and made much of him. Comonfort was a good, well-meaning man who believed totally in the politics of compromise. The adulation he received convinced him all the more firmly that the program of the new government must be watered down so that nobody could be offended. The moderates convinced General Álvarez that he was the cause of the recent revolts, and for the peace and welfare of the country, he must step down, and let Comonfort take his place.

Álvarez could have borne the slights and snubs he had endured during his brief weeks in office. He could not, however, bear the thought that he might be the cause of further turmoil in his country. He resigned and, turning his back on the morass of snobbery and opportunism in the capital, started the long ride back the way he had come, back to his *tierra*, his land, in Guerrero.

Melchor Ocampo, disgusted with Comonfort's vacillations, had already resigned. But Juárez knew that his *Ley Juárez* needed shepherding, and defending. He had watched with sorrow the withdrawal of the staunch and truly liberal Álvarez. He understood and he regretted Comonfort's weakness. But the important thing was the law, so he chose to remain with the government. When a combination of army and clergy in Oaxaca rebelled against the Juárez Law, and Comonfort asked him to take a small force of soldiers back to his home state and quell the uprising in order to enforce the law there, Juárez went.

It had been almost three years since he had been home.

10

NEW LAWS AND
A NEW HOPE

Oaxaca and Mexico City
1856-1858

The newly appointed Governor Juárez had not quite reached the city of Oaxaca—in fact, he had got only as far as Etla, where he had been seized by Santa Anna's troops three years before—when he was met by an enormous crowd, who cheered his arrival and accompanied him all the way into the city. Once there, he was greeted by a salute from the city's cannon. It was the rebels' way of showing that they bowed to his authority.

Thus Juárez entered into another brief period of accomplishment for his state, and of happiness with his family. Once again he knew the contentment of being at home, of hearing the church bells sounding from all parts of the city, of seeing the hills of Monte Alban, still green from last summer's rains, and the familiar rugged outline of his own sierra.

His first acts were to reorganize and make more efficient the National Guard, to stock the armory with guns and ammunition, and to initiate classes in military science at the Institute. He had learned, these last few years, that ideals were not enough. They must be secured against military onslaught. He also established a liberal newspaper, which Mexico's leading journalist of the period called "the best newspaper in the Republic." He founded a hospital, built another school for the training of teachers, established a mint which used local metals and proved an enormous aid to the miners of the area. He took the dispensing of charity out of the hands of the church and instead created a system of public welfare where recipients were no longer treated like charity cases but like self-respecting citizens.

And unlike previous governors, who had always appeared at affairs of state and public gatherings in elegant uniforms and gold-braided, pseudo-military hats, Juárez made his public appearances dressed as always in his plain black frock coat. Nor did he follow his predecessors' custom of having armed and uniformed sentries on guard at their homes. Instead, he abolished the guard altogether. He was a citizen like any other, living contentedly at home with his family.

During his second year as governor the national government promulgated two documents which would profoundly affect Juárez's life and the history of his country.

The first, published early in 1857, was the *Ley Lerdo,*

a companion to the *Ley Juárez*. As Juárez's law had diminished the extralegal privileges of the church, the Lerdo law tried, in a tentative way, to weaken the church's stranglehold on the Mexican economy.

One of Mexico's most serious problems was that most of the vast holdings of the church lay idle and unproductive year in and year out. And because these lands and mortgages had been willed to the church in perpetuity, no one else had the right to buy them and put them to use. Mexico's secretary of treasury, Miguel Lerdo de Tejada, a mestizo born in Veracruz, was anxious to end this situation, and to stimulate the farming and economic life of the country.

He was no radical, however. He was a strong believer in the rights of individual ownership, and did not want to strip the church of its property without remuneration. His position was rather like that of some northerners in the United States who, at that moment in history, opposed slavery but did not believe in abolition. They believed their government should *buy* the slaves' freedom, so the slaveholders would not be out of pocket.

Similarly, under Lerdo's law, no land would be confiscated outright; but henceforth the church could own only its church buildings. Its vast lands were to be put up for sale at prices deemed fair by the Mexican government. In addition, a sizable tax would be placed on each sale, which would bring money into the government coffers. The new law would apply to land owned by any corporation, but the church lands were Lerdo's primary target.

Passage of the *Ley Lerdo* precipitated another clerical uprising in Puebla and brought the church close to revolt in other parts of the country. The new constitution, published a month later, proved even more inflammatory.

For a year, delegates had been meeting in Mexico City to work out a new code of laws which would eliminate the defects of the old. Most of the delegates were lawyers, Catholic, and moderate in their politics. It was not a radical document which they worked out. It made no mention of freedom of religion, but neither did it give the church a continued monopoly on religion in Mexico. This alone was enough to bring condemnation of the document from every high church officer up to the Pope himself. But the church also objected to the rights of public education, freedom of opinion, freedom of the press and of assembly, and of course most particularly to a restatement of the Juárez and Lerdo laws. Many of the documents' provisions were derived from the United States' Bill of Rights, but this mattered not at all to the clergy, who would rise in insurrection rather than permit the separation of church and state in Mexico.

On the other hand, there were liberal delegates who objected to the new code because it did not go far enough. Ponciano Arriaga, one of Juárez's former companions in exile, rose to deplore the fact that the constitution gave the people a number of theoretical "rights" but made no mention of their most pressing problem—poverty. "The Constitution should be the law of *the land*," he said. "But the condition of the land . . . is not even considered. Are we to practice popular government and have a hungry, naked and miserable people?" The Mexicans, he said, could not be free or republican, in spite of a thousand laws proclaiming abstract rights, until they had access to the soil and the tools to till it with.

Arriaga's prophetic complaint, however, was lost in the storm of abuse the church heaped on the document.

A final draft was approved at last, and according to its provisions every public official was required to swear an oath of allegiance to the new code. First to swear fealty was the aging Dr. Gómez Farias, who was carried into the hall on a pallet and helped to kneel, the other delegates following suit. Within days, the church announced the excommunication of every official who had so sworn. Not one of them could receive the sacrament, or a religious marriage, or a Christian burial.

At this pronouncement, many public servants resigned their offices. Others stayed on, but lived in a torment of anxiety at finding themselves in conflict with their church.

At *Pascua*, Easter Sunday, President Comonfort went to the great cathedral on the zócalo to worship, and was denied entrance. And soon after, in Oaxaca, Benito Juárez learned that his reelection as governor would not be solemnized with a Te Deum in his city's cathedral, as had been the custom since the birth of the republic.

Word had reached Juárez that the clergy hoped he would order soldiers to break open the doors of the cathedral and arrest the priests, thus starting off his new term of office with an act of violence.

But this was not Juárez's way. He decided that it was high time the functions of church and state be separated even in customary rituals. The people should have proof, from their government, that no one religion was favored over any other. So he was sworn into office in a civil ceremony, and vowed to uphold the constitution of the republic. There was no further reference to the clergy.

Oaxaca had one other proof of Juárez's determination that civil law should supersede church law. The parish priest of a little Oaxacan village had been called to attend the deathbed of the local mayor. But the mayor, like all public officials, had sworn allegiance to the new constitution, and was therefore an excommunicant. So the priest had refused to give him the last rites, or to allow his burial in the churchyard.

Juárez promptly ordered the arrest of the priest, and advised the Bishop of Oaxaca that the village stood in need of a priest to replace him.

It would not be long before church and state would meet in final combat.

By the summer of 1857, elections had been held, and Comonfort's moderates had won a majority of the seats in the nation's legislature. Comonfort was reelected, and Benito Juárez was elected chief justice of the supreme court, a post which carried with it the right of succession to the presidency in case of emergency.

Somehow Comonfort seemed to sense that such an emergency might arise. He wrote Juárez that he was appointing him minister of the interior as well. This post would give Juárez authority over all matters dealing with public security, local uprisings, and the police. "You will also help me calm certain ambitions on the part of the liberal family that are dangerous in this difficult crisis we are passing through," he wrote. But most of all, because of Juárez's knowledge of the whole situation, he wanted him at his side, "should it be necessary for you to *take upon yourself the supreme command of the nation* [italics author's], in the event of the failure of my health or some other serious occurrence. . . ."

Juárez had not wanted to be a nominee for the chief justiceship. The cabinet post was only a further complication. But it was his nature to serve when called upon to do so. He appointed an interim governor to replace himself in Oaxaca, and late in October he set out for the capital.

The rains were over now, and the roads passable, but he left his family at home. Perhaps he, like Comonfort, correctly read the temper of the country, and knew that there could be physical danger in store for anyone connected with the government in the mercurial city of Mexico.

November 1 was the "Day of the Dead," when Mexicans gathered at the burial places of their families, chatting and drinking, and eating the "cake of the dead." The custom was to leave the food that remained for the spirits of the deceased to eat when everyone had gone home. From twilight on, the suffused light of candles, illuminating the carpets of marigolds strewn over each grave, gave a soft orange glow to each village churchyard; and the murky smoke of incense made it all seem strange and unreal, as though seen in a dream.

Juárez, weary from a week on the road as his horses pressed forward, must have passed several such scenes on his last evening of travel en route to the capital. Up ahead loomed the dark shapes of mountains which guarded the valley of Mexico. Here at hand a churchyard, with its pools of smoky orange glow, could have intruded but dimly on his consciousness as he looked ahead and wondered what he would find tomorrow, when he descended those mountains into the nation's capital. What, he must have wondered, lay in wait?

11

DISORDER

Mexico City, Guadalajara, and the Countryside 1857-1860

Juárez arrived in Mexico City to find the capital a hotbed of rumors about an impending coup d'état. It was known that Comonfort had become unhappy with the long list of civil rights guaranteed by the new constitution. He had asked the legislature to suspend it, and the deputies had refused. Comonfort was an honest man, but in his earnest desire to please everyone, he was unable to please anyone. In addition, he was under heavy pressure from the church. He was deeply devoted to his mother, and she in turn was equally devoted to her priest and confessor, Father Francisco Miranda, who was one of the most militant clerics in all Mexico.

The coup was not long in coming.

In mid-November Comonfort held a secret conversation with several men who were in bitter opposition to the constitution, including a reactionary general named Félix Zuloaga. All the men, for different reasons, felt the Mexican people were not yet ready for self-government. On the first of December, Comonfort was again sworn into office as president, and before two weeks had passed, the impending coup was an open secret.

On December 15, Juárez was summoned to appear before Congress. The lawmakers had heard that General Zuloaga was involved in a conspiracy, and they were worried that there might be others in the army implicated as well. When Juárez appeared before them, they asked whether his department was prepared to deal with a possible uprising.

Juárez told them the bald facts. The government could count on the loyalty of only about three thousand troops. The safest measure, he said, was to proceed with tact and caution before arresting Zuloaga.

As he left the hall after his appearance, he was told that the president wanted to see him. Comonfort took him to a small office off the mezzanine where they could be alone. Juárez realized that his chief was extraordinarily nervous and excited, as though he expected to meet with some sort of vigorous opposition. Comonfort burst forth with a recital of his troubles under the present constitution and blurted out, at last, that he was going to change his role in Mexican politics.

Juárez sat quietly, observing the harried former liberal

who had drifted so far from his ideals. "I knew something," he then admitted. "But since you had said nothing to me, I did not want to say anything to you."

"Well," said Comonfort, "I am saying something now." He told Juárez of his and Zuloaga's projected coup against the constitution, and urged him to join them.

The little Zapotec sat calm, unruffled. "Choose whatever path you like," he said, "because I have already chosen mine." He wished Comonfort luck, but said he would not go with him.

That night, Comonfort received from the other conspirators a revised plan for the revolt, far more reactionary than that to which he had previously agreed. When he finished reading it, he sank back onto his sofa in dismay. To a confidant who was with him he said, "I have just exchanged my legitimate title for that of a miserable revolutionary! . . . But what is done, is done. *No hay remedio." There is no help for it.* A tragic phrase, so often used in his country.

The next night, Zuloaga's soldiers entered the city and took possession of it. When Juárez went, dutifully, to the National Palace to work the following day, he was seized, and held prisoner there.

But now Zuloaga and his fellows demanded that Comonfort resign. The unhappy president refused. He freed Juárez from captivity and called his own troops into action against Zuloaga's. Once again the streets of the city resounded with gunfire, bullets spat from windows and rooftops. But the president's troops were overcome, and in mid-January 1858, Comonfort, who had entered the city as Mexican democracy's best hope, traveled wearily out of it, to Veracruz and from there to exile.

The liberals who had helped him form his government also fled for their lives. For the most part, luck was with them. One was sheltered in the American consulate, one escaped disguised as a muleteer, and another hid among bundles on a pack horse.

As for Juárez, he was trudging along on foot across the farmlands to the northeast of the city. By night he slept in the fields. By day he pressed on. He managed to catch a mail coach, which took him to Querétaro, but within hours that city too had declared for Zuloaga. A few days later he reached the mountainous mining town of Guanajuato, where almost half a century earlier, Father Hidalgo's ragged band of rebels had stormed the granary and captured it from the Spaniards. And here, in legal succession to Comonfort as president of the country, Juárez announced the reestablishment of Mexico's legitimate government.

He was joined by Melchor Ocampo and the young poet Guillermo Prieto, and other liberals. An army, under the still loyal general Anastasio Parrodi, was on the move. Parrodi wanted the shadow government to move to a more defensible location, and at his urging, they went on to the bustling colonial town of Guadalajara, in the state of Jalisco.

Word reached them there that Parrodi had met the

rebel forces and been badly defeated, with heavy losses in men and material. Juárez reacted to the news philosophically. "Guillermo," he said to Prieto, "our rooster has lost a plume."

The defeat came closer to home the following day.

Juárez and Melchor Ocampo and a few others were together in the state buildings when a group of soldiers, led into mutiny by the local clergy, came storming into the building shouting, "Long live the army! Long live religion!" Juárez, Ocampo, and some sixty or seventy government officials were herded into one long room and held captive. Guillermo Prieto was imprisoned elsewhere, but he sought out the rebel commander and demanded that he be imprisoned with his president. For his pains, he was knocked down and kicked in the head. When he came to, he found himself in the long room with his fellows. Juárez was deeply moved by the young man's fidelity. Ocampo, like an affectionate older brother, upbraided him for not having tried to escape.

Outside, they knew, all was pandemonium. The rebel soldiers had opened the jails and freed the prisoners to fight the loyal forces. The city echoed with the sound of rifles.

Next day, a rebel squad came charging into the state building. They appeared at the door of the room where Juárez and the others were imprisoned, raised their rifles, and the leader cried, "Aim!"

Juárez reached for the handle of a nearby door as if to sustain himself, then raised his head and waited. But

Prieto threw himself in front of Juárez, protecting his chief's body with his own. Just as the leader cried "Fire!" Prieto called out, "Put up your arms! Brave men are not assassins!" The rifles wavered. Prieto's words poured forth. Afterward he could not even remember what he had said, but the would-be assassins stood bewildered, listening. Prieto turned to one old soldier and cried out, "You want blood? Take mine!" The old man, shamed, lowered his rifle, and weeping, others did likewise.

Then it was all over, the soldiers vowing they would not kill the prisoners. Juárez embraced Prieto and the others all crowded round the young man, calling him the savior of the Reform.

A few days later the mutineers released their prisoners, and Juárez and his fellow officials set out for safer terrain. The rebel army, however, was hot on their heels.

In a little town named Santa Ana Acatlán, Juárez learned that their enemy, with a vastly superior force, was about to close in on them. He suggested that the rest of his "government" flee, and that he remain to share the fate of his soldiers. But no one would abandon him, and in the middle of the night the whole group moved out of the village. They continued their march for days. Juárez's fifty-second birthday saw his arrival at an hacienda where the Indians greeted him with drums and flowers, crying, "*Viva* Juárez!"

En route once again, more bad news reached them.

Parrodi had surrendered his entire military force without a battle. Juárez's whole army now consisted of 350 men and two cannon.

Days of journeying up mountain ranges and down into valleys brought them to the tropical port of Manzanillo on the Pacific. Here they waited for a boat to take them to Panama.

They were a travel-worn, bedraggled group, referring to themselves as "the sick family." Prieto, who was really ill, had never seen the ocean before, but hadn't the strength to walk down to look at it. Juárez and Ocampo made a chair of their hands and carried him out onto the phosphorescent sand of the shore, an excursion Prieto recalled years afterward: ". . . I, riding proud and triumphant," he wrote, "with my soul singing in my breast, happier than on the first throne of the world!"

At last their boat came. It carried them down the steaming coast, to Acapulco, and then finally to Panama. They traveled by rail across the isthmus, and then by boat again to New Orleans, where the former exiles showed Prieto the shabby hotel in which they had stayed before, waiting out their exile, rolling cigars for a living and dreaming of Mexico. Prieto described years later how his friends looked to him on this visit: "Juárez . . . his clear and serene brow, his black eyes full of sweetness, his impassive countenance. . . . Ocampo with his great mane of hair, and his round face and his snub nose, and his large but eloquent mouth, and his winning speech. . . ."

The visit was brief. It was time to take the boat again, for Veracruz.

12

THE WAR OF THE REFORM

Veracruz
1858-1861

As a ship approaches Veracruz, the first glimpse of land is the peak of Orizaba, a perfect cone, rising snow-capped almost twenty thousand feet. Somewhat lower is the massive, blunted Cofre de Perote; below that the green of tropical growth, and finally the sun-baked city with its palm-fringed shore and teeming harbor. Juárez's packet arrived at a good time. It was May, the weather was hot, but the terrible *nortes* had not yet begun to blow. As the ship moved past Juárez's old place of confinement, San Juan de Ulúa, its massive cannon gave him a twenty-one gun salute.

The band played, the governor made a welcoming speech, the Veracruzanos cheered wildly. It was a homecoming to warm the heart. Juárez and his official "family" repaired to their quarters, and Juárez gave proof that he was still a "son of the people."

Finding there was no water in his room, he sought out a servant to ask for some. Assuming that the stocky, rather shabby little Indian was the president's houseboy, the woman sharply ordered him to get it for himself, and Juárez, good-naturedly, obeyed. But when she saw him next, in the dining room, and heard the others address him as "*señor Presidente*," she ran out of the room, crossing herself in confusion.

One could have a sense of physical security in this bustling little harbor. Guarded by malarial swamps and abrupt mountain slopes at its back, and the sea at its front door, Veracruz seemed to offer assurance that here at last the refugee government of Mexico could defend itself. Trade by sea was brisk, munitions could be brought in, and revenue from the customs-house would help pay long-overdue salaries for soldiers and members of the government. Best of all, wives who had long been separated from their husbands could think of joining them here.

Far to the south in Oaxaca, Margarita Maza de Juárez decided to make the journey with her family. The oldest of her eight children was fourteen, the youngest still a babe in arms. They could not go by carriage over the roads because rebel troops might recognize and harass them. So, while the summer's downpours alternated with its scorching heat, they set out on foot, along trails and footpaths, down the gullies and up the mountains of the sierra, journeying almost three hundred miles to reach Veracruz, and Juárez.

The family had been safely reunited for several months when, near the end of 1858, there was another coup d'état in Mexico City. The brilliant but reactionary general Miguel Miramón seized power from the adventurer Zuloaga, and embarked on a far better-organized campaign against the liberal forces. Early in 1859, he directed an attack against Veracruz by land.

His soldiers moved down the mountains, and bivouacked near the swamps. They quickly found themselves in battle not only against the Constitutionalist (liberal) soldiers, but against the anopheles and the *Aedes Aegypti* mosquitoes as well, though they did not know, of course, either the names or the peculiar potency of these insects. Soon combat casualties were joined by malaria and yellow fever victims, and Miramón's soldiers were forced to withdraw. Quiet settled momentarily over Veracruz.

But it was not so in the environs of the nation's capital. The liberal general Santos Degollado, preparing for an attack on Mexico City, had deployed part of his troops at Chapultepec, and part in the hilly suburb of Tacubaya. They were, however, attacked by the rebel general Leonardo Márquez and roundly defeated.

Márquez was not satisfied with victory alone. He not

only executed all his prisoners, even dragging the wounded out of their hospital beds, but shot as well the doctors who were attending them, and countless of the soldiers' wives and children. For this act of savagery he became known, to Mexico and the world alike, as the "Tiger of Tacubaya."

By now, both sides were hard-pressed for money to fight the war, and Juárez took a step which he had long known was necessary. The Lerdo law had proved to have serious limitations. In an effort to strengthen the rights of private property, the law had forbidden not only the church, but any corporation whatever, to own large holdings of land. This resulted in the forced sale of many *ejidos*—those village-owned lands set apart since early Spanish days for the use of the villagers. The loss of these lands caused severe hardship for the Indians.

Equally serious, however, was the fact that church and other lands put up for sale were so vast and expensive that the poor could not afford them. Instead, wherever the law was enforced, great tracts of land were being bought up by foreigners and the already wealthy. The proceeds from these sales were of course going back to the church, which remained as rich and powerful as ever.

So, in July 1859, Juárez issued his Decrees of Reform, confiscating all but the church buildings themselves and breaking up the huge holdings so that small landholders could afford to buy. The cemeteries were nationalized, and Mexicans would henceforth not be forced to pay the church for burials, marriages, or registry of birth. In addition, there would be absolute freedom of religion.

However, it was one thing to issue decrees; it was another to enforce them when much of the country was in rebel hands.

The rebels were still winning victories. From the outset they had had behind them the church's wealth and the military skills of most of the country's best generals. On Juárez's side were the Indians and the mestizo ranchers, who believed so strongly in the liberal cause that they simply would not accept defeat. When they were overcome, they withdrew, disappearing into the mountains, to come back and harry the rebel forces another day.

All the troops tended to live off the land, using a sort of "scorched-earth" policy. Time and again *campesinos* saw their little plots of farmland overrun by soldiers, it mattered not of which side. Their produce was "liberated" to feed the troops, and their huts were burned. As during the American war and the war of Santa Anna, no matter who won, the *campesino* lost.

And as the fighting went on, rebels and government forces alike became more reckless in their search for funds. Both sides—but most particularly the rebels— began seizing foreign holdings: mines, land, a silver train. Miramón obtained a small loan from France, putting up as security an enormous number of worthless bonds which he could have had no intention of redeeming.

And at one point, Juárez's government became so desperate for money to pursue the war that Juárez considered ceding to the United States the whole of Lower California, together with strategically located strips of land for American railroads. However, this suggestion evoked such furious protests on both sides of the border that the negotiations came to nothing.

Foreign governments were using the desperation of the embattled country to wrest trade advantages for themselves and to charge usurious rates of interest for loans. They threatened to intervene to obtain settlement for their seized and damaged property. England and France pressed for a compromise government that would guarantee them indemnities.

Juárez's government in Veracruz, beset by all these pressures from home and abroad, hung on stubbornly. During the winter of 1859 to 1860, they faced another attack from Miramón's forces.

This time Spanish ships moved into the harbor, menacing them from the sea, and rebel forces ringed the city from behind, subjecting it to a relentless bombardment. For three weeks, cannonballs wreaked destruction and death on the city. The hideous black vultures that constituted the city's street-cleaning department were busy indeed.

But the city would not surrender. Once more, the rebel forces withdrew, and within four or five months the tide began to turn. Constitutionalist forces, out in the countryside, began to recapture land that had been in rebel hands for almost three years.

Strangely, now that victory was within sight, some of the Constitutionalists seemed to lose the will to fight on. General Santos Degollado urged Juárez to compromise with the rebels. Juárez promptly removed him from his command, replacing him with Jesús González Ortega. Others in Juárez's cabinet suggested that a peace be worked out even if it meant sacrificing the constitution. This Juárez would not do. He listened quietly and courteously to all the suggestions, and continued the war.

At last, toward the end of 1860, the rebel forces sustained a crushing defeat near Mexico City. Miramón realized that all was lost. He, Zuloaga, and other rebel leaders divided up a large sum of money seized from British bondholders in the capital and quietly made their escape. Miramón fled to Europe, and the others into the all-concealing mountains.

The dispatch about the final battle reached Veracruz when Juárez and Margarita were at the opera, two nights before Christmas. Juárez ordered the music silenced and the curtain lowered, and he read aloud the news of the end of the civil war.

The audience went wild. The opera singers burst into an emotional rendition of the *Marseillaise*, the French national anthem. In light of what would soon happen to Mexico, the song was at once a comic and a tragic choice.

On New Year's Day, 1861, the snow-capped peaks of Popocatepetl and Ixtaccihuatl looked down over a city turned almost mad with excitement.

At the head of his twenty-five thousand loyalist troops, General González Ortega rode triumphantly into the capital. Passing a downtown hotel, he chanced to see his predecessor Santos Degollado on the balcony. Amid the band music, the shouting, and the rain of flowers, he insisted that Degollado come down to join him. He gave him an affectionate *abrazo* for his part in the victory, and they finished the parade riding side-by-side.

Ten days later, Juárez rode into the city in his almost severely plain, black carriage. He was dressed, as always, in his black frock coat. His entry was suitably modest. The fighting was over and the constitution saved, but the country was well-nigh in ruins and he knew there was much to do.

13

THE VULTURES HOVER

Mexico City
1861

Mexico was penniless. Previous wars and spendthrift presidents had left a legacy of debt. During the war of the last three years both sides had borrowed heavily from European powers. Foreign holdings had been seized, foreign property damaged, and the owners held Juárez responsible for Miramón's debts.

And the countryside was ravaged. Márquez, Zuloaga, and other rebel leaders were still preying on the liberals from their mountain fastnesses, while in the capital, the reactionaries who had fought with or supported the rebels were another problem. What was to be done with them?

At the conclusion of United States' own civil war four years later, Americans would hear President Lincoln deliver his second inaugural address, in which he would urge the combatants of both north and south to construct a just peace: "With malice toward none; with charity for all . . . let us strive on to finish the work we are in; to bind up the nation's wounds. . . ." That, too, was Juárez's wish: to bind up *his* nation's wounds, and declare a general amnesty for the defeated rebels.

But just as the Reconstruction in the United States fell tragically short of Lincoln's hopes, so the Mexican citizens and press demanded revenge on the rebels. Congress attacked Juárez for dealing too leniently with them. It was not enough to have won the war. Armchair generals who had discreetly sat out the war now wanted the blood of the vanquished.

Certain precautions for the survival of the government itself had already been taken. The bishops who had fomented rebellion had been exiled. Wealthy landholders who had supported the rebels were stripped of their lands and banished, as were certain foreign diplomats who had conspired against the constitutional government. A few political prisoners were awaiting trial, but for the most part, in spite of public pressure, Juárez's decrees of amnesty prevailed.

Against considerable opposition, Juárez was reelected that spring. His new cabinet included many of his loyal supporters, but not his old friend Melchor Ocampo.

Ocampo had gone home to his *rancho* in Michoacán. During that April and May, Juárez had frequent letters from him. They were warm, happy letters about his daughters, his "little harvest of wheat and corn," and a wine he had discovered, made from the wild grapes of a nearby valley. It seemed during those few weeks that after all his wanderings in support of Juárez and his cause, Ocampo was at long last able to relax and enjoy living.

But on June 2, Juárez received worrisome news. Guerrilla followers of Márquez, the "Tiger of Tacubaya," had appeared at Ocampo's hacienda and dragged him away, no one knew where.

Juárez had two anxious days of waiting for news, and then, early on the third morning, he was wakened by a messenger who brought him the tragic story.

As the guerrillas' prisoner, Ocampo had been taken on a three days' ride to an inn about forty miles from Mexico City. There the group of riders had halted. Ocampo had been given pen and ink, and was told to write his will. To a priest who offered to confess him, he said, "Father, I am well with God, and He is well with me." Then, guarded by ranks of armed and mounted guerrillas, he was taken a little distance from the hacienda, ordered to dismount, and shot. The assassins hung his body from a tree.

When this news reached Mexico City, the people stormed the presidential palace, demanding immediate execution of all political prisoners in reprisal. Juárez refused. He ordered extra guards at the jails, to make sure the prisoners would not be dragged out and lynched by the mob, and announced to the aroused citizens that the prisoners were under the protection of Mexico's laws. No matter what the assassins had done, he stated, he was "governor of an enlightened society."

But in the countryside, the outrages continued. Before the month was out, General Degollado too had been seized and assassinated, and the bullet-riddled body of another much-loved young liberal general, Leandro del Valle, was found pinned to the trunk of a tree. It was a dragon's harvest. As each hideous act was succeeded by another, it only served to point up Mexico's helplessness. She could not even pay for soldiers or arms to keep the peace.

There was almost no way to turn. Mexico was trying to pay off her debts. Most of the revenue from her custom-house was already going directly to England, France, and Spain. But funds were also needed to keep the government alive and functioning.

Juárez decided that the needs of his people must come first, and in mid-July, he did the only thing possible. He declared a two-year moratorium on the payment of all foreign debts.

There was an instant, and furious, reaction from abroad. France threatened invasion. Britain wished an "authoritative interference on behalf of order." Translated, this meant she wanted to seize the customhouses at Veracruz and Tampico until the British debt was paid. Spain still dreamed of her old empire, but would settle for a forced payment on her debts.

And Mexico's powerful neighbor to the North? For the first time in decades, there were men in office who were not passionate advocates of Manifest Destiny. President Lincoln and many of his appointees looked upon Mexico not as a country to be devoured piecemeal, but as a young democracy struggling for existence.

However, the one weapon which could have brought American military might to Mexico's aid, the Monroe Doctrine, could not be enforced. The United States was embroiled in civil war. The week that Juárez had declared his debt moratorium, the first battle of Bull Run had been fought. From then on, moral support was all that the United States could offer Mexico, and that was not enough. The embattled little republic lay like a wounded animal, waiting for the predators to come in for the kill.

They were not long in coming. Although in autumn Juárez asked Congress to repeal the moratorium, his move came too late. In November, Spanish warships sailed into the harbor of Veracruz.

They were, everyone knew, merely the first. French and British troopships were hastening to join them.

On December 15, 1861, Congress granted Juárez emergency powers to deal with the intervention. An English journalist chanced to be sitting that day in the gallery of the long room in the National Palace where Congress met. He had been unfavorably impressed by the "frumpery" of the room and the "riffraff" sitting near him in the gallery. But then, amid a blare of trumpets, Juárez came in.

"He is a dark, small man, quiet and self-possessed," the Englishman wrote, "affectionately known in Mexico as 'the little Indian.' . . . A very respectable, well-meaning man, and of fair talents . . . and he deserves very great credit for his firmness and tenacity in maintaining the struggle and the cause of legitimacy. . . . On taking his seat, he bowed gracefully on all sides, and immediately made the following address in a clear and remarkably pleasant voice."

Juárez thanked Congress for the powers it had granted him, noting the terrible responsibility such powers carried with them. He hoped, he said, for a peaceful settlement with the three European nations. But if this hope were thwarted, then he counted on the nation to defend its revolution and its independence.

Thus ended, for Juárez and Mexico, the year 1861. It was a year that had seen Juárez's entry into the capital as legally elected president, his desperate struggle to avert bankruptcy for his country, the loss of his best and most devoted companion, Melchor Ocampo, and the brutal assassination of other Mexican heroes. At this moment in its history his country was too poor even to defend itself by sea. The Spanish fleet had been able to sail unmolested into Veracruz harbor and disgorge six thousand men, whose presence was still unexplained by Spain.

It had been a hard and bitter year. And there was little hope that the following year would not be even more disastrous. What Mexico did not realize, however, was that the arrival of the Spanish troops was merely the opening gambit in a French despot's move for empire in the New World.

14

INTERVENTION

Veracruz, Puebla, and Mexico City 1861-1863

Napoleon III had been on the French throne for ten years. He was a dedicated Catholic, and he yearned to equal the achievement of his uncle, Napoleon Bonaparte, in giving France an empire. His wife, Eugénie, was no less ambitious. And the imperial couple had for some time been exposed to the blandishments of the Mexican expatriates.

Mexico's exiled bishops had found their way to the French court, as had a few long-since-discredited Mexican royalists and several of the émigré landowners. Among the expatriates were Juan Almonte (reputed to be an illegitimate son of Father Morelos), who had been an associate of Santa Anna; Gutiérrez Estrada, a royalist since his young manhood; and José Manuel Hidalgo, a ladies' man whose vast holdings in Mexico had been confiscated by the liberals. Together they had convinced first the empress, and then the French monarch himself, that Mexico was a country of great wealth, and that it was only Juárez's cupidity, or his incompetence, that could account for the country's inability to meet her debts. The people of Mexico were good Catholics, they said, who groaned under the tyranny of the Reform laws and yearned for a Catholic monarchy to put things right.

The French emperor could use a military adventure at that moment, to divert his people's attention from internal problems. Too, he had an illegitimate half-brother the Duc de Morny, who added fuel to the fire. De Morny had bought up millions of francs' worth of those defunct Mexican bonds and was eager to profit on his investment. Most inflammatory of all was France's pompous, alcoholic, and irascible ambassador to Mexico, the Comte Dubois de Saligny, who had sent home reports to His Imperial Majesty that Juárez was "an idiot and a rascal," that the Mexican people were all thieves, and that the government was in the throes of "social decomposition." When one or two timid voices were raised to the contrary, no one listened. And Juárez's suspension of payments on foreign debts gave Napoleon the pretext he needed. He wanted the debts settled, yes, but what he really wanted was Mexico.

One of the Hapsburgs, Austria's ruling family, was suggested as a candidate for the throne of Mexico. Accordingly, the royalist Gutiérrez Estrada, with the sanction of Napoleon III, traveled to an isolated castle on the

Italian shore of the Adriatic to offer the throne to Archduke Maximilian. The archduke was a gentle, serious young man of twenty-nine, with a fair beard, a fine-featured face, and a head full of liberal ideals.

There, amid the gardens planned by Maximilian's young Belgian wife, Carlota, looking out over the incredible blue of the Adriatic, the most tragic figure of the whole French intervention was drawn unsuspecting into the plot.

Maximilian was a younger brother of Austria's emperor Francis Joseph. He had led a pleasant, sheltered life which had not equipped him for the ruthless world of politics. He believed Estrada's story of a nation longing for a return to church and monarchy. He believed Estrada's assurance that England and Spain would support him, and perhaps—who could tell?—even the United States! The young archduke dreamed of bringing a better, happier, and more devout life to the people of Mexico. But not, he said, unless he were truly wanted. He said he would take the throne at the expressed desire of the Mexican people.

While he awaited such evidence, an agreement was signed in London by France, Spain, and Great Britain, arranging for a joint occupation of Veracruz, in order— or so Britain and Spain thought—to force Mexico to pay its debts. The Spanish fleet was at that time in Havana, and, therefore, had been the first to arrive. In early January of 1862, more ships from Europe sailed into the harbor, putting ashore seven hundred British marines and twenty-five hundred French soldiers. And still, none of the Allies had bothered to give Juárez a clear explanation for their presence.

The Mexican army, ill-equipped and having no support at sea whatever, withdrew to a more defensible position at Cerro Gordo. Below, on the seacoast, the foreign troops swarmed over Veracruz and the adjacent countryside. They soon began to feel the effects of the desert plains and fever-breeding swamps near their bivouac. The officers wrote Juárez asking for permission to move their troops to healthier ground.

Juárez wrote back courteously, saying that such approval could only be granted if the Allies would pledge themselves to respect Mexico's constitution and her territorial integrity. The Allies agreed, thereby conceding Juárez the right to represent his country in negotiations, and were allowed to move up to the cool green plateaus and hillsides of Córdoba, Orizaba, and Tehuacán.

Britain and Spain presented their demands against the Mexican government. They were fair demands, and Juárez's emissary Manuel Doblado promised that every effort would be made to meet them. As negotiations proceeded, the Spanish emissary's sympathies began to swing markedly toward Juárez and his cause. The British envoy wrote home that Juárez and Doblado represented "the best reflection of public opinion to be found in this unfortunate country." "Juárez," he continued, "is still

looked up to as embodying a principle which the liberal
party fought a three years' war to maintain."

But the French ambassador dealt his allies an unpleas-
ant surprise. He denied ever having agreed to respect
Mexico's independence or Juárez's presidency, and presented a demand for twenty million pesos' indemnity, a
demand so patently unjust that the envoys of England
and Spain were astonished and outraged. They began to
realize they had been tricked, and that the debt was
merely France's excuse to violate Mexican soil. Angrily,
they washed their hands of the whole affair and began
their withdrawal.

But French troops were now arriving in force. They
were offered support by Márquez, the "Tiger of Tacubaya," and his tatterdemalion army. Juan Almonte arrived from France to declare himself provisional president. These were hardly impressive additions to France's
"army of liberation," and French soldiers began to wonder where the *rest* of the Mexicans, who were reputedly
so eager to be liberated, were keeping themselves.
They soon discovered.

General Lorencez's crack French troops, marching
through the wooded highlands toward Mexico City,
reached the plains and hills of Puebla. The clean and
charming colonial city, with its tile-studded churches and
its pleasant, even streets, was within sight. Two fortified
hills guarded its approaches. Serene and snow-capped,

four volcanic peaks looked down on the marching columns.

But in moats and ditches, and behind the rows of maguey cactus which serve Mexican *campesinos* as boundaries for their little plots of land, the Mexican army was waiting.

Lorencez's men charged straight up the fortified hills into the mouths of the Mexican guns. Helped by a torrential afternoon rain that turned the hills into unscalable mud slides, the Mexicans turned back the invaders three times. By day's end the French had lost five hundred men and were in orderly retreat, back toward Orizaba.

It was the fifth of May, 1862. Mexico's soldiers, scorned by their experienced and arrogant enemies, had triumphed gloriously. Small wonder that they would declare it thenceforth a national holiday, the *Cinco de Mayo*, to celebrate with pride a battle they won, in a campaign they lost.

Before the battle of Puebla, General Lorencez had written home to the emperor, ". . . at the head of 6000 soldiers, I am already master of Mexico." After his retreat, however, he wrote home again, asking for fifteen to twenty thousand more troops. He realized that the émigré royalists, the Mexican bishops, and most of all France's embittered minister to Mexico, Comte de Saligny, had misrepresented Mexico's true strength and the force of her republican ideals. In fact, Lorencez wrote, a monarchical party in Mexico simply did not exist. He had yet to find a single member of such a movement.

But the French emperor was too deeply involved to withdraw. And it was easier to believe what he *wished* to believe. He was eager to combat the spread of the dangerous democratic ideas that were cropping up all over the globe. He wanted to prevent the United States from gaining control over the Caribbean and the Atlantic shores of Central and South America. And he was convinced that the Mexican mines would make France rich. He removed General Lorencez from command and sent over thirty thousand fresh troops under General Frédéric Forey, with instructions to listen more closely to his oracle, the minister de Saligny.

Not all Frenchmen were deceived. Novelist Victor Hugo wrote from exile that his sympathies were entirely with Mexico. And a French historian, excoriating his nation's policy, wrote, "Under absolutist government, to cover the initial error has always been called, '*saving the flag*' [italics author's]." He warned Napoleon III of a fate similar to that of his uncle's: "Because of these senseless enterprises . . . you [Bonapartes] have perished once before under the wrath of the world and dragged France down with you in your ruin. . . . Learn from your own history!"

Most French newspapers, however, chose, as did the emperor, to believe the slanderous lies of de Saligny. They carried on a campaign of abuse against Mexico's culture and people, and they reserved their most furious attacks for her president. From Mexico City, Juárez issued statement after statement insisting on his country's right to determine her own destiny. But across the Atlantic, his words were largely ignored.

It was a sad and difficult time for the Juárez family that summer. Their baby daughter Amada died. And from Oaxaca came word of the death of Margarita's father, don Antonio Maza, who more than four decades ago had given refuge to their cook's twelve-year-old brother, Benito Juárez.

And in Veracruz, Mexico lost its hero of the battle of Puebla, young General Ignacio Zaragosa, dead of typhoid. Juárez, anxious to heal old wounds among his countrymen, called former president Comonfort back from exile, and gave him Zaragosa's command. In the months to come, Comonfort would have the chance to fight, and at last, to die, for the constitution he had helped make and then tried to destroy.

Autumn saw the arrival of the new French general with his troops. Nature, as though in defense of embattled Mexico, treated the invaders to a never-to-be-forgotten *norte*, a north wind which all but tore Veracruz apart, crippling eleven French boats in the harbor and making disembarkation impossible for days.

When the French did come ashore, they found themselves greeted as anything but liberators. Shops closed in protest against their presence, and women went to church in mourning. The hideous black vultures of the area crouched on housetops and tree limbs, glaring balefully at the new arrivals. They seemed an ominous portent indeed.

Until the end of 1862 and through the beginning of the following year, the French were hounded by bad weather, fever, the "black vomits," and a shortage of food, fresh water, and transport. They were bogged down for weeks in Veracruz. The few miles to Jalapa and Perote seemed like thousands. Many officers felt as though they had been caught in quicksand. They found fault with their general, and the ordinary soldiers found fault with the war itself. They began to suspect they were going through all this misery for the benefit of the holders of those defunct bonds.

The invaders' snail-like pace inland gave Mexico time to brace itself for a second attack on Puebla. At the year's end Juárez visited the city to make sure everything possible had been done to fortify it. Puebla guarded the road to Mexico City; the French must be stopped here, or the capital itself would be next.

The bulk of Mexico's army was brought up to meet the expected arrival of the enemy. On a gloomy day in mid-March, the advance squadrons of the French came into view. And the day after, a day which broke brilliant with sunshine, the inhabitants of Puebla could look out and see the enemy army spread out, twenty-six thousand of them, magnificently dressed and impressively armed, on the hills and plains surrounding the city.

The French encircled Puebla with their cannon, completely cutting it off. On March 21, they began a systematic bombardment.

There was street fighting, too, on the outskirts of the city. But every house had been fortified, and Mexican guns behind garden walls and on rooftops answered the French guns. The French tried to take the city block by block, but as one French officer wrote home, "The Mexicans are defending themselves with a vigor we did not think them capable of." Baffled, the invaders drew back and settled down for a long siege.

The bombardment went on daily, filling the Puebla streets with rubble and taking a tragic toll of soldiers and inhabitants. But at last a still graver danger became apparent: food supplies were giving out. Before long, the people were eating their dogs and cats.

And then the ammunition ran out.

The siege had lasted eight weeks. For Mexico's general González Ortega, there was now no alternative. He destroyed what remained of his weapons, and surrendered. His men poured out of the city, almost naked and close to death from hunger, to be taken prisoner by the French.

The Mexican royalist Almonte wanted them shot on the spot, all twelve thousand of them. But the French command refused. The men were fed. Some were pressed into the traitor Márquez's army. The officers were sent to Veracruz for shipment to France, and most of the soldiers were sent to the coast to work on the railroad.

When the French moved into Puebla, they were met by utter silence. They were hated. They could take no pride in their victory, because in the end it had been starvation, not military might, that had conquered the city. A French captain wrote bitterly in a letter, "We shall be masters as usual only of the points we occupy. After eighteen months of war, we shall have conquered the road from Veracruz to Mexico City." And so far, that was all.

In the nation's capital, Juárez was now faced with a grave decision. His army consisted of only fourteen thousand men. France's army was twice that. The approach from Puebla was now vulnerable. One could put up a glorious defense of the city, but defeat and the loss of the rest of the army were almost certain. Was the glory worth it?

And which was more important, the capital, or the nation?

In the long run, glory weighed less with Juárez than common sense. He decided that the government should withdraw to the north, build its strength, and fight another day.

On May 31, 1863, the Assembly convened in the National Palace and gave Juárez a vote of confidence. In mid-afternoon, the great cannon of the palace boomed out the announcement that the Assembly was dissolved, and people began to swarm across the zócalo, to gather in front of the National Palace, some curious, some sombre. Many were carrying their children.

Juárez oversaw the removal of important national documents and made sure that all was orderly and in readiness. At the usual hour of sundown, the flag was lowered.

The crowd in the zócalo had swelled. They stood in silence, watching, waiting. Juárez and his ministers stood on the balcony, where the palace overlooked the zócalo.

As the flag came down, drums rolled, troops presented arms, the army band played the national anthem. Lights were beginning to come on in the buildings about the plaza. The cathedral's lacy facade was fading into the twilight.

The flag was brought to Juárez. He received it, put it to his lips, and cried out, "*Viva México!*"

The crowd answered him with one voice.

The next day the palace was empty, and the city waited for its conquerors.

15

OCCUPATION

San Luis Potosí, Saltillo, Monterrey 1863-1864

The entry of the French troops into the capital was carefully prearranged. There was a glittering parade, the clergy turned out in force, and there was a suitable number of "ecstatic" Mexicans to throw flowers under the feet of the invaders. The French army later billed the French government for the flowers.

But when the tumult and shouting died down, and the flowers were swept up, the Mexican clergy received a rude surprise. Former church holdings, it appeared, would not be returned to the church, but would continue to be the property of the wealthy landowners who had bought them. One cleric's protests were silenced with a threat of guns.

With that question cleared up, the French representatives got quickly to work on the matter of a provisional government. There would be a triumvirate, it was decided, which included the royalist Almonte (whom nobody wanted), the Archbishop of Mexico (who wasn't there), and a rather anonymous third gentleman whom one French officer described as "a mummy who has been unearthed for the occasion." There was even an Assembly of sorts, which would be allowed to choose any sort of government for Mexico so long as it were a monarchy.

The monarch himself was still in Europe. Maximilian was approached once more, and he repeated his willingness to accept the throne if the Mexican people indicated by plebiscite that they really wanted him. It was now up to the French army of occupation and their Mexican collaborators to "liberate" enough of the countryside so that a plebiscite could be held.

Meanwhile, on the fertile central plateau to the north of the capital, Juárez and his cabinet, as well as his wife and children, had settled in the mining center of San Luis Potosí.

Juárez's family was increased, now, by the marriage of his oldest daughter, Manuela, to a young Cuban writer, Pedro Santacilia, one of Juárez's companions-in-exile during the New Orleans period. In the troubled days to come, Juárez would find his new son-in-law an indispensable ally. This was fortunate, because he was discovering there were few others upon whom he could rely.

The liberals were losing battles. Discouraged, old

friends and supporters were falling away. Juárez suspected that Santiago Vidaurri, one of his generals and a powerful political leader in the northeast, could not altogether be trusted. Indeed, the French were making a concerted effort to bribe a number of Juarist generals, and in some cases, they succeeded.

Those generals who were still loyal to the republic were seriously hampered by lack of supplies. Juárez's minister in the United States had been able to buy limited amounts of armaments there and get them smuggled past Confederate border patrols. But the guns were reconditioned, and many of them fell apart the first time they were used.

Still, Juárez did what he could to keep his storm-tossed government on an even keel, and among his few blessings these days he could count the valor and faithfulness of Ignacio Comonfort, who was now his commander-in-chief.

Since the former president's arrival from exile, he had thrown himself devotedly into the defense of the liberal cause. In November 1863, he visited Juárez in San Luis Potosí to discuss the campaign with him. On the morning of his return to headquarters he had risen early, before his staff were up and about, and in the stillness of the early dawn, found himself in conversation with the poet Guillermo Prieto, who was a guest in the same house.

It was one of those rare, quiet moments, when friends speak of what is most important to them, and when they are singularly sensitive to each other's moods. Comonfort talked of his dreams for the salvation of Mexico, and of his deep affection and respect for Juárez.

Prieto, aware of the dangers lying in wait for all the soldiers of the republic, put his hand on Comonfort's neck. "Take care of it," he said.

Comonfort smiled. "The little Indian takes care of that," he said.

But before a week had passed, Comonfort was ambushed by reactionary soldiers on the road from San Miguel de Allende. They killed him, stripped his body, and left it lying in the road.

The French and their Mexican cohorts had been continuing their advance northward. By now they were all too close to San Luis Potosí, and Juárez knew he must send his family out of harm's way. There were many hazards involved in such a journey. Wartime was a dangerous time to be traveling, and in that still wild countryside there was always the additional danger of bandits. Both Margarita and Manuela were expecting babies, and Juárez's second son, José, young Pépé, had not been well. A journey would be taxing for all of them. The French, however, were a still greater danger and so Juárez dispatched his family, in Santacilia's care, to Saltillo, not far from the northern deserts. He lived through days of anxiety until he had word that they had arrived safely.

A month later, just before Christmas, he too was on

his way to Saltillo, and San Luis Potosí had fallen to the French.

In Saltillo, troubles continued to mount. Juárez had no sooner arrived, in mid-January of the new year, than two of his generals sent messages asking him to resign "for the good of the country." Jesús Gonzáles Ortega had been Juárez's supreme commander during the war of the Reform. He was an able military man, but vain and ambitious. The other general, Manuel Doblado, had also fought valiantly during the same war, but had often given Juárez cause for concern because of his impetuosity and lack of judgment. In their messages to Juárez now, they argued that the French would never make peace as long as Juárez represented the Mexican government.

Juárez's answer was that the nation had given him his post in trust. He could not surrender it, he said, without betraying that trust. Such an act would plunge the republic into chaos. And the French might not accept Ortega either, or any other Mexican who opposed the intervention. Their whole aim in Mexico, he pointed out, was to establish a government useful to France.

He thanked the two generals for their concern and assured them that he would continue to do everything in his power to help his country in the defense of its independence and its dignity.

Time would prove the accuracy of Juárez's instincts.

By midsummer, Doblado lost his will to fight. He resigned his commission, had one wild night of celebration in the border town of Matamoros, and left for the United States where he died the following year. Ortega went on to fight for the republic until he too tired of losing battles. His conduct at a later date would reveal what his real motives had been that January in Saltillo.

Indeed, the new year of 1864 brought little fresh hope to the liberal cause. To be sure, Porfirio Díaz still held Oaxaca, and from the tropical wilds and mountains of Guerrero, the old guerrilla Juan Álvarez sent this call: "I still live, men of the coast—I, who have ever led you against tyrants!"

But the liberal general José López Uraga had gone over to the French. And Juárez's fears about Vidaurri proved correct. A large deployment of government troops managed to keep him from delivering his troops to the French, and he had fled over the border into the States. The seaport of Tampico and all of Yucatán were in enemy hands. And along the central plateau, the French were still pushing north.

By now, Juárez and his family had moved on to the mining and industrial center of Monterrey. Margarita had just delivered their last child, a boy, and their first grandchild was a month old. But Juárez knew that for their own safety, he must once more send them away. He took time out from his official duties to buy a dress for his *viejecita*, his little old woman, and one blistering August day, helped get his family aboard carriages. It now consisted of his wife, his nine children, his infant granddaughter, and the indispensable Santacilia. He rode with them as far as the little town of Cadereyta, where he bid them good-by. Every human being he loved in the world vanished into the empty reaches of the northern desert. For almost four months, he did not know if they were alive or dead.

The French meanwhile, having captured most of the populous central plateau, had obtained something vaguely resembling a plebiscite on the accession of Maximilian. Not exactly a *vote*, the French commander wrote home apologetically, because in most of the countryside there was no list of voters. Besides, the Indians wouldn't really have known what the vote was about. Therefore, a few royalist dignitaries in every city or town had "assumed" how the local Indians *would* vote if they understood the issues, and had arrived at a grand total of about six and a half million (out of a total of eight million) in favor of Maximilian. The young archduke had been formally notified, and on April 10 he announced from Miramar that he accepted the call to take the throne of Mexico.

He and Carlota boarded the frigate *Novara* at Miramar and sailed down the Adriatic and around the toe of Italy's boot. Then they continued on up the Mediterranean coast, pausing at the ancient port of Civitavecchia. From there they traveled to Rome for the Pope's blessing on their venture.

But Pius IX surprised them with a stern warning about the church's former holdings in Mexico, which the French had refused to restore to the clergy. "Great are the rights of the people, and it is necessary to satisfy them," said His Holiness, "But still greater and more sacred are the rights of the Church!"

With this warning ringing in their ears, the imperial couple returned to their ship and set off once more, to leave behind them the familiar blue waters of the Mediterranean and to sail across the darker Atlantic, toward the New World and their waiting subjects.

16

EMPIRE

Mexico City and the North
1864-1865

During the long sea-crossing, Maximilian composed a letter to Juárez. He was convinced that all Mexicans, including Juárez himself, would collaborate with him gladly once they understood that he had their interests at heart. His letter, therefore, urged the president to meet with him in the capital to discuss Mexico's problems. The empire, he said, would show its respect for Juárez's years of service by placing him in "some distinguished position."

This done, the emperor-to-be spent the rest of the crossing preparing a book of court procedure and etiquette for his new subjects.

The *Novara* reached Veracruz at the end of May 1864. Maximilian and Carlota had been prepared to expect a glorious welcome when they went ashore, but there was no one there to meet them. Puzzled and deflated, they returned to their ship and slept aboard that night.

Next day, Almonte came hurrying into Veracruz with profound apologies. But even the official reception was cold. The Veracruzanos had had three and a half years to learn to dislike anyone sent over by Napoleon III. Maximilian and Carlota survived the chill greeting, took a carriage, and began their journey toward the capital. The carriage broke down and they had to borrow another. It was not an auspicious beginning.

Still more disturbing was the letter Maximilian received from Juárez in answer to his cordial letter from shipboard:

His surprise was great, Juárez wrote, to read that Maximilian had come in response to a "spontaneous summons" from the Mexican people. He had thought Maximilian would have recognized an invitation issued by a handful of discredited royalists and exiled clerics as merely some ridiculous farce. "Frankly," wrote Juárez, "I have suffered a disappointment. I thought you one of those pure beings whom ambition could not corrupt."

The president refused the invitation to Mexico City with all its assurances of protection because, he said, Napoleon III had broken so many treaties that the word of his agents could not be trusted. Juárez concluded his letter with these words:

"It is given to men, sir, to attack the rights of others, to take their property, to attempt the lives of those who

defend their liberty, and to make of their virtues a crime
and of their own vices a virtue; but there is one thing
which is beyond the reach of perversity—the tremendous
verdict of history. History will judge us. I am
>"your obedient servant,
>"Benito Juárez."

As Maximilian pondered this astonishing communica-
tion, he and Carlota and their party continued on their
way over the unspeakable roads leading from Veracruz.
However, by the time they came within sight of Puebla,
the local clergy had managed to prepare a show of welcome, and when the royal couple reached Mexico City
they were altogether reassured.

An apartment had been prepared for them in the National Palace. Neither of them got much rest the first
night, however. There were so many bedbugs that His
Imperial Highness took refuge on the billiard table, and
they decided to move to other quarters as soon as possible.

Their choice fell on Chapultepec Castle, where less
than two decades before young Mexican cadets had
hurled themselves to death rather than surrender their
flag to the invading Americans. To be sure, the castle
was by no means as elegant as Miramar, or the palaces of
their royal childhoods, but it boasted landscaped rooftops
and terraces, and looked out over a sea of tall cypresses
and Indian laurel trees. From its battlements one could
see, below and beyond, the ancient, beautiful arches of

the aqueduct that led toward the heart of the city, and toward the southeast, the two snow-capped volcanoes standing tranquil watch over the entire valley. When the castle was remodeled and the young empress had furnished its *sala* with gold-brocaded Louis XV furniture and two pianos, its wardrobes *à la chinoise,* and its baths with warm-hued Italian marble, it was a dwelling not to be ashamed of.

The young couple quickly acclimated themselves to the customs of the country. They took to wearing the native sombreros when they went riding and serapes against the cold. Carlota went to mass in a lace mantilla. They even learned to eat, and enjoy, Mexican food. In exchange, French bakers taught Mexican *panaderos* to build ovens of iron or brick and bake hard-crusted French rolls, as an alternate to the omnipresent tortillas.

Soon after his arrival, Maximilian took a tour of the "liberated" portion of the countryside, visiting mines, jails, and hospitals, while Carlota acted as regent in the capital. The imperial couple made every effort to please their new countrymen.

They did not really understand them, however. It was impossible for the young emperor and his wife to comprehend the steady, intransigent desire for freedom that burned in the hearts of men like Benito Juárez.

When Juárez had written his letter to Maximilian, the republican government had been stationed in Monterrey.

But the French were nearing the city and Juárez had known he would not be there long.

Soon after his family's departure, in August 1864, he was having dinner in his quarters when a band of Mexican turncoats invaded the city's streets in anticipation of the arrival of the French. Juárez's associates urged him to make a rapid escape. Once before in this same city, when urged to take to his carriage and flee a group of insurgents at a gallop, he had answered, "At a trot. The President of the Republic cannot run." So now he calmly finished his meal, got into his old black carriage, and amid a hail of bullets, drove away.

A few miles out of town one of his battalions caught up with him and escorted him and the other government officials on their way. A wagon bearing the nation's archives trundled along after them. The soldiers and the motley collection of vehicles made for Saltillo, but before they could reach it they had news that it, too, had fallen to the French.

Juárez managed to find a place to hide the archives, in a cave in the countryside not far from Saltillo. Then he and his party continued their pilgrimage. Often hungry, oftener thirsty, they made their way for long, weary days and nights through the hideous heat of the northern deserts. By now, the French were taking over more and more of the area and there was almost no place safe for the weary travelers. At last, late in October, they reached

Chihuahua, where they established temporary headquarters.

It was two more months before Juárez received the word he had been waiting for so anxiously. Late in December Santacilia wrote that the Juárez family had reached New York City and were living on East Thirteenth Street. They had lost young Benito Jr. for a few anxious hours in New Orleans en route, and their baggage had disappeared altogether. But at least Juárez knew that they were safe and well.

Or were they? Perhaps Santacilia knew something he had been reluctant to tell Juárez, not wishing to give him more cause for worry during those days when Mexico seemed to be in its death throes. Several more weeks elapsed with no news from New York. When at last Juárez did hear, it was not from his son-in-law, but from Matías Romero, his minister to the United States, who had just visited Santacilia in New York. "He informed me," wrote Romero, "of the grave condition of the son of the señora."

Few words, but coupled with Santacilia's silence, they conveyed much. Juárez sensed instinctively what they meant.

He wrote Santacilia. He understood, he said, that in his letter Romero had only been trying to break the news gently, that at the time Romero had written, "really, my Pepito did not then exist—does not now exist—isn't this true? You will understand all that I suffer by this irreparable loss of a son who was my delight, my pride, my hope. . . . Excuse the blots, because my head is lost. Juárez."

Three more weeks passed with no word of confirmation or denial. Juárez fluctuated between the conviction that he had lost his beloved second son and the hope that everything was all right. He wrote Romero a long letter excoriating some of their countrymen who thought Mexico should cede certain territories to the United States in exchange for military aid. "The enemy may come and rob us," he wrote, "but we do not have to legalize that crime, handing over voluntarily what is demanded of us by force!" But by the letter's end, he was a father again. ". . . I cannot say more, because the death of the son I loved so much presses with such a dreadful weight on my heart. . . ."

Late in February Romero wrote him, confirming what Juárez had read between the lines. Pépé was dead.

Nor was there anything in the military situation to lift the weight from his heart. Oaxaca, his *tierra,* his own land, had fallen to the French. General Porfirio Díaz and his twenty-eight hundred men had fought stubbornly against an enemy army of ten thousand. French cannon had been mounted on the hills of Monte Alban and had subjected the city to weeks of steady bombardment. Finally, food and ammunition exhausted, Díaz had surrendered and was now in a military prison. Juárez's only grim satisfaction, on hearing this news, was the knowledge that Maximilian would have to leave a large body of troops in occupation there, to keep the freedom-loving Oaxacans pacified.

There was little to celebrate, least of all his fifty-ninth birthday. Nevertheless, the people of Chihuahua gave him a surprise dinner on the twenty-first of March, and he found himself at the head of a table having to make a speech.

It was a brief one. He told his listeners that it was a great good to give one's life for one's country and that "as men we are nothing; principles are everything." A local official offered a toast to Juárez's wife and children. It required almost more courage than Juárez could summon, to reply. "I see the country here," he said, with difficulty, "and I say to it solemnly that my sacrifice is nothing, that the sacrifice of my family would be much, would be infinite for me; but if need be, so be it."

He sat down, in tears.

17

A GILT COACH AND A PLAIN BLACK CARRIAGE

Mexico City and the North
1865-1866

The old year had ended with a hint of conflict to come between Maximilian and his former sponsors, the clergy. The monarch still refused to take the former church lands from their new owners and restore them to the clergy. Even worse, he was planning a series of reforms to give Mexicans religious freedom, when late in 1864 the Pope's nuncio, Monsignor Meglia, arrived from Rome. Maximilian must, he insisted, restore the church's holdings. In addition, the Holy Father would not tolerate the existence of any form of worship in Mexico other than Catholicism. He would not sanction the burial of non-Catholics in the country's cemeteries, nor permit any teaching whatsoever, public or private, except under the church's guidance. Even the sale of Protestant Bibles was to be prohibited. After all, it was the Holy Church that had created the empire!

Maximilian realized with a shock what Juárez had long known—that members of the clergy had actively conspired to overthrow not only Juárez's government but previous ones as well; that then as now they had contested "the legitimate authority of the state." However, he vowed, "good Catholic that I am, I shall likewise be a liberal and just prince."

It would not be easy.

In addition, the well-meaning emperor had embarked on an economic policy which, though he had yet to realize it, could lead only to disaster. Believing in the unlimited supply of Mexico's mineral riches, he had committed himself to repaying not only Mexico's outstanding debts to France, but also the cost of food, billeting and pay for the vast French army of occupation. In addition, he was faced with the cost of carrying on the war against the Juarist forces and the paying off of those millions of dollars' worth of discredited bonds. He had also begun to spend money liberally in refurbishing Chapultepec Castle and in entertaining there, and he had plans to build a wide and stately boulevard from his residence to the National Palace. When he drove to the government offices in the morning in his beautifully fitted carriage with its gold-leaf trim, it would be agreeable to travel along an avenue like the ones he had been accustomed to in his youth, with grassy circular islands spaced along the way, with pillars and monuments and rows of trees.

Actually, if one included the enormous interest rate charged by banks and speculators in France on money previously advanced, Maximilian had already more than tripled Mexico's foreign debt. But he was not unduly concerned. He was confident that all Mexico's problems could be solved by the superior wisdom, experience, and efficiency of her European masters.

If Maximilian was not worried, however, Napoleon III had begun to be.

All was not going well with the United States. That is to say, the Confederacy (which Napoleon supported) was losing, and in the spring of 1865, Napoleon realized he might soon find himself with a victorious Union army on Mexico's northern border.

The Union would not take kindly to a large body of undigested Europeans in the western hemisphere. Napoleon knew he must achieve total victory quickly, or not at all. He instructed the French commander-in-chief, now General Achille-François Bazaine, to consolidate his positions for a final push against the Juarist forces.

But Bazaine discovered that whenever he pulled his troops out of one area to move them to another, republican troops or guerrillas moved in. It was like trying to stem the tide.

Early in autumn a rumor reached the capital that Juárez had fled across the border. On the strength of this story, Bazaine persuaded Maximilian to declare that the republican cause no longer existed, and that from then on, anyone raising arms against the imperial forces would be declared a bandit and executed on the spot. "This is a war to the death," Maximilian wrote, at his general's prompting. "A war without quarter between barbarism and civilization. On both sides it is necessary to kill or be killed."

The new decree did not frighten Juárez's supporters into submission. On the contrary, the war took on a more savage character. Soldiers of both sides went sweeping through the countryside, punishing the inhabitants if they were so much as suspected of being sympathetic to the enemy. If a villager was caught with arms in his possession, he was put to death and his hut burned. Each act of cruelty brought its act of reprisal. In one jungle area the villagers were forced to take to the trees to escape Bazaine's forces.

Scores of republican military and government officials were captured and executed, but their followers fought on. In November 1865, the frustrated Maximilian received news that was even more serious. He was informed that an agent of Napoleon III had approached the United States Secretary of State William Seward, asking for recognition of the Mexican Empire in exchange for a gradual withdrawal of French troops.

This would leave Maximilian's government virtually unprotected, in a land hostile and still unpacified. It was now Maximilian's turn to be worried.

He had learned, to his cost, that the Mexican exiles in Europe had lied, not only about Mexico's vast mineral

wealth but also about the strength of the Catholic movement. He had learned, too, like Juárez, that the word of
Napoleon III could not be depended upon. Maximilian
was in grave danger of finding himself altogether alone
and defenseless.

From his temporary quarters in hot, dry Chihuahua,
Juárez had watched the progress of the United States'
Civil War with concern, knowing how closely Mexico
would be affected by its outcome. "I celebrate and ap-
plaud the inflexibility of Mr. Lincoln," he had written
earlier. But he was too much of a realist to hope for
substantial aid from the Union. It was enough that the
North destroy slavery and not recognize Maximilian. In
April, when news reached Juárez's headquarters of the
terrible event at Ford's Theater in Washington, it was a
profound blow. Lincoln, Juárez wrote, "who worked
with such constancy for the full freedom of his fellow
men, merited a better fate than the knife [*sic*] of a cow-
ardly assassin."

Meanwhile, at home, Bazaine's forces were threaten-
ing Chihuahua, and once again Juárez and his government took to the road. There were more days of travel
over dusty desert land, under the relentless sun, until
they reached the Rio Bravo (known on the other side of
the border as the Rio Grande), and the little town of El
Paso del Norte.

The day they arrived, a young American customs offi-
cial-turned-correspondent chanced to be on the Mexican

side of the river. He had been lulled almost to slumber by the somnolence of the village when suddenly the whole place sprang to life and people on all sides of him were shouting, "Juárez is here!"

The young man had, in his short life, met and known a number of American heroes, Lincoln and Grant among others, and his respect for them had survived undiminished. He watched now as the dusty caravan of wagons, barouches, and an old black carriage pulled up. He saw Mexico's president dismount: a short man, with a dark, Indian face and a quiet, scholarly appearance. The American observed his thoughtful manner of speaking and listened to his singularly clear, sweet voice. During subsequent days, the correspondent had the opportunity of getting to know him better, and he wrote, "The longer I knew and the more I studied him, the more was I impressed with the greatness and goodness of his character."

As for Juárez, he could stand here in El Paso del Norte (afterward to be renamed Ciudad Juárez) and look across the river toward an American town on the other side, and know that it could offer him sanctuary. Yet he refused to leave his homeland. It was important for his people to know that he would not leave.

He stayed through that blistering summer and the autumn that followed. He was facing a difficult decision.

This year, 1865, would normally be an election year. But how could an election be held? Mexico was a war-torn country. The constitutional government itself was in flight most of the time, trying to evade the French forces. At best there were only a few scattered areas, totally isolated from each other, which were still loyal to the government.

On the other hand, according to the constitution, if an election were not held at the proper time, the presidency must pass automatically to the head of Mexico's supreme court, in this case, General Jesús González Ortega, and Juárez knew the general well enough to know this would mean chaos and anarchy. Most of the republican governors would not support him. Even the military would be hopelessly divided. And Ortega, Juárez was afraid, was capable of any treacherous accommodation with the enemy. He "belongs to the school of don Antonio López y Santa Anna," Juárez wrote his son-in-law.

Ortega had, early that spring, made a tactical withdrawal "for military reasons" across the Texas border, and had chosen to remain there. Now, from the safety of North American soil, he was bombarding his homeland with pronouncements and propaganda against the president.

For Juárez it was a tragic predicament. Every political instinct he possessed warned him not to allow Ortega to succeed to the presidency. He had spent his whole life trying to uphold the principle of government by law, yet if he upheld the law in this instance, it would mean the end of the republican cause. What was he to do?

While he was struggling to come to a decision, he had

news from New York that his fifteen-month-old baby Antonio had died.

It was almost more than he could bear. But terrible as it was for him, what must it be for Margarita? Grief-stricken and desperate with anxiety about his wife, he wrote Santacilia begging him to give her support and comfort.

They were hundreds of miles apart at this moment, but he had known Margarita since her childhood and knew what she could bear and what she couldn't. As he feared, this last disaster was almost too much. Margarita's letters, when they began to reach him, were all but incoherent. Months later, there was still anguish on every page. "The loss of my sons is killing me," she wrote him. "From the moment I awaken I think of them, remembering their sufferings, blaming myself, and believing that it was my fault they died. . . . This remorse is killing me. I find no remedy, and the only thing that calms me for a few minutes is the thought that I shall die, and I prefer death a thousand times more than life. My present life without you and without my sons is insupportable. . . ." "When the children see me crying, they can only do the same. . . ." "I do not wish to afflict you, but it consoles me to tell you of my sufferings. They would anger a stranger, but you will not be angry, you will be kind. . . ."

As winter came on, it was growing increasingly evident that the tide had turned for the republican forces.

The United States government was putting increasing pressure on Napoleon to withdraw his army. American officers friendly to the Juarist cause were bringing large quantities of armaments to the banks of the Rio Grande, "condemning" and dumping them, and making sure that republican forces knew where to find them. Local recruits, heartened by republican victories throughout the countryside, began to swell the ranks. In Puebla, Porfirio Díaz managed to escape the convent where he was held prisoner, and made his way south to join forces with the guerrillas of old Juan Alvarez.

Juárez, biding his time in El Paso del Norte, could be pleased at this news, but his political dilemma was costing him several of his supporters, including the poet Guillermo Prieto, who had saved his life in Guadalajara. The ambitious González Ortega had exploited Prieto's devotion to the constitution, causing a rift between the two old friends. Prieto tried to patch matters up, but Juárez was curt with him. He had been through too much to be tolerant of Prieto's doubts and fears.

Nor had he time to regret the lost friendship. It was one of the fortunes of war—and politics. "Better alone," he wrote Margarita philosophically, "than in bad company."

Early in November, he found a way out of his dilemma. He decreed that any republican officer who remained abroad without government permission was considered a traitor to the cause. This disposed of Ortega's claim and extended his own term of office until peace would make a new election possible.

With almost no exceptions, the Republican generals and governors throughout the country approved his act. But the rift with Prieto was beyond repair.

Meanwhile, Napoleon III was finding the Mexican situation increasingly untenable. His near neighbor Prussia, under the leadership of Otto von Bismarck, had become a serious military threat. As Juárez observed, Bismarck had "stirred up the wolves of Europe." All those French battalions in the New World might find themselves badly needed at home.

Also, the United States was growing increasingly impatient. In March 1866, Secretary of State Seward again demanded French withdrawal from Mexican soil, and stationed General Philip Sheridan on the Texas border with fifty thousand men to make sure Napoleon took the demand seriously.

Long ago, Seward had been an aggressive advocate of Manifest Destiny, but that was not why he was rattling the sabre now. And although the presence of the French army was clearly a violation of the Monroe Doctrine, even that was not the whole story. If the French army withdrew, French landholders and mine owners would go with them, and American capital could rush into the vacuum. As Seward was coming to realize, his countrymen now "wanted dollars more and dominion less" than in earlier days.

In response to Seward's pressure, Napoleon agreed that he would withdraw a third of his army in November, and the remainder in March and November of the following year. It seemed a simple military agreement. Actually, it was Maximilian's death warrant.

18

THE MAN WHO MEANT WELL

Mexico City and the North
1866-1867

Maximilian's predicament was almost insoluble.

He knew that to keep up the war against the republicans required soldiers and money. But the treasury was chronically bankrupt and the soldiers were going home. The foremost French financial experts had been unable to solve Mexico's economic problems and the country was no nearer peace than it had been when he arrived.

The Emperor had become honestly fond of his new country and its people. He knew where many of its sicknesses lay. Of course some of his army officers, and sometimes even Carlota, complained impatiently that the only solution for Mexico's troubles would be to get rid of all the Mexicans and repopulate the country altogether. But there were others among the French who recognized the basic evil. As long as peonage existed, they said, there could be no progress. Peonage was not a new evil.

Since the Spanish conquest, the life of an Indian who belonged to an hacienda in Mexico was worse than that of a slave. "I have seen men beaten until they bleed," wrote one French engineer. "I have fed families dying of hunger and driven to work by the lash of the overseer. . . . The landowner speculates even on the food of these poor people, and on the rags that half-clothe them. He makes them buy all their food from him, and at a higher price than in the public market. . . . The Indian is driven deeper and deeper into debt. . . ." And the debts, of course, were passed on to the sons when the fathers died.

But when Maximilian issued edicts against the system he alienated his last bastion of support, the conservative landholders. The edicts were quietly buried, the ills went uncorrected, and Maximilian was now opposed by both the clergy and the conservatives, the very people who had brought him to power.

He and Carlota tried to forget their troubles by taking vacations at their summer home in Cuernavaca, in the lovely Borda gardens. They tried to heal their unhappiness at Carlota's childlessness by adopting the little grandson of Agustín de Iturbide, Mexico's self-declared emperor of almost half a century before. But every day brought fresh worries and frustrations, and at last, that summer, Maximilian decided to abdicate.

But Carlota was proud, and the increasing tensions of their predicament were making her strangely moody and hot-tempered. She would not let him admit defeat. She would go to France herself, she said, and make a personal appeal to Napoleon not to withdraw his troops. As always, Maximilian bowed before her determination.

She left Veracruz in July, and it was quickly apparent to those on shipboard that her behavior was erratic. The sound of the motors upset her. She could not sleep. She felt as though there were a tight band around her head.

In Paris, Napoleon himself was ill and when Carlota reached France he tried to postpone seeing her, but she would not be fended off. She managed to force an interview, and then a second one, during which Napoleon wept, Eugénie sobbed, and Carlota railed. But to no avail. "It is all slime," she wrote Maximilian, "from beginning to end!"

She went to Rome, hoping to persuade the Pope to bring pressure on Napoleon in support of her husband. At the Vatican, as in Paris, she argued brilliantly, but again to no avail. And this time, the emotional shock of another failure was too great. She became haunted by the thought that Napoleon's agents were trying to poison her and refused to drink any water unless she herself had drawn it from the fountains in the Rome piazzas. In a few days' time she was storming the Vatican again, totally distraught, demanding that His Holiness protect her from the French emperor's hired assassins.

Her brother was sent for and took her to Miramar, but even the tranquil vista of flower-filled gardens beside the blue Adriatic could not restore her. Finally, hopelessly mad, she was brought back to her family in Belgium. Nor was she ever to recover.

The news reached Maximilian in October.

He went into seclusion, and when he emerged, he had reached a decision. Once again, he announced he would abdicate. He closed up Chapultepec Castle, and set out for Veracruz. But on the way he stopped at his second vacation home, in Orizaba, and lingered there, uncertain. He tried to distract himself by studying botany and entomology. He caught butterflies and classified them, and he tried to decide what to do about the throne.

The announcement of his decision to abdicate had roused a frantic protest, this time from members of his cabinet and from Gutiérrez Estrada (who had not even come home during Maximilian's reign, but had remained comfortably abroad). Many other Mexican royalists who, although they frowned on his liberalism, were even more afraid of the republican government that would follow inevitably in his wake, also pressed him to remain.

On the other hand, the French general Bazaine and Napoleon's personal envoy to Mexico, Edouard de Castelnau, urged him to sue for peace and to replace himself with any popular republican leader save Juárez, stipulating only that the French debt be acknowledged. This, they pointed out, would spare the nation further conflict and would allow the French army and Maximilian himself to retreat with dignity from an impossible situation.

At the last, it was Maximilian's pride and conscientiousness as a Hapsburg that tipped the scales. He could not abandon the people who had supported him. On the first of December he announced that he would remain on the throne of Mexico, with or without the French army. While Bazaine and Castelnau fumed, he returned to Mexico City to resume his imperial duties.

The two Frenchmen knew that only disaster could follow Maximilian's decision. They tried to make a private arrangement with Porfirio Díaz. They would deliver the capital to him with only token combat, if he would disclaim Juárez. But Díaz refused. Early in 1867, in a last desperate effort to force Maximilian's capitulation, they destroyed all that remained of the French army's arms and ammunition. But not even then would Maximilian agree to abandon his empire.

On February 5, 1867, Maximilian stood in a window in Mexico City, watching the last of the red-trousered French troops march out of the city. "At last," he said, "I am free!"

Free of the French, yes, but still caught in currents that would carry him inexorably toward final tragedy.

And Juárez knew it. He understood his country and its people so well that he could almost predict what would happen to Maximilian. He had a calm, clear view of events that kept him from indulging in wishful thinking, and he had as well a steady faith in the eventual triumph of justice and democracy.

Through much of 1866 he had remained in the northern outpost of El Paso del Norte, living an almost spartan existence and endlessly occupied with the movements of his various armies. He tried throughout to maintain some sort of cohesion among the widely scattered areas of the country now under republican control. "He is a man patient and persevering beyond all others," wrote Castelnau to Napoleon, "who knows so well how to wait!"

It was a hard year both for Juárez and for Margarita and the family. He had drawn no salary for more than a year. There simply was not enough money in the coffers to cover even his most basic needs. In August, the soldiers of General Mariano Escobedo's army took up a collection and sent the president five thousand dollars as a gift. He returned it with his thanks and continued to make do as best he could.

Margarita, accustomed to a life of considerable penury in New York, had found herself rather surprisingly the center of much attention that spring. She had gone to Washington to nurse the aged and ailing mother of the Mexican ambassador Romero. As soon as American officials discovered her presence there, she was invited to a presidential reception and to a formal dinner at Secretary of State Seward's house. She was shocked to read afterward in a local paper that she had appeared "elegantly dressed, with many diamonds." "That is not true," she wrote Juárez. "All my elegance consisted of a dress that you bought me in Monterrey shortly before I left. . . . And as for the diamonds, I had no more than some earrings that you gave me once on my Saint's day. . . . I tell you all this because they shall not say that when you were in El Paso in such poverty, I was there enjoying luxury. . . ."

Ever the devoted wife, she ended her letter with a reference to Juárez's possible journey to Chihuahua later in the year. "I am fearful of your having to pass nights in the desert during the winter; take care of yourself as well as you can."

She was glad when the public appearances were done with, and a few days later wrote again the words that occurred so often in her letters to him: "I shall have peace only when at last I am with you."

By summer, victories of the Army of the North made it possible for Juárez to board his old black carriage once again, and return to Chihuahua. Along the way the villagers greeted the arrival of the vehicle with cheers and churchbells.

The Atlantic port of Tampico was republican now, as were the Pacific ports of Guaymas and Mazatlán. Monterrey was once again firmly in republican hands, and by autumn they had also recaptured the important city of Guadalajara. The old black carriage, which had become a symbol of the sweep of the republican forces through the interior, reached Durango the day after Christmas. Juárez and Margarita could begin to make plans by mail for the return of the family to their homeland.

In January, Juárez proceeded to the old Spanish mining town of Zacatecas, perched high among the hills, and the inhabitants gave him a noisy welcome of fireworks. But soon after his arrival, the imperialist general (and former president) Miramón attacked the town with a sizable body of soldiers.

Urged to leave the city at once, Juárez decided instead to remain with the republican troops. The inhabitants had greeted him with such wild enthusiasm that he did not want to discourage them. He stayed on until it became clear he would have to flee or fall prisoner. Then he and his ministers left the city on horseback while Miramón sent his cavalry in a frantic chase after the presidential carriage, which was hurtling quite empty along a different road.

A week later, with Miramón's men forced out of the city again, Juárez returned, to find that an important enemy document had fallen into the hands of the republicans. It was an order from Maximilian to Miramón telling him that if Juárez and his ministers were captured, to try them by court-martial, but to communicate with His Imperial Highness before executing them.

Did it imply that Maximilian would have granted Juárez a chance to renounce the presidency in exchange for his life? Or that Maximilian wished to pronounce the death sentence himself, as an example to the republicans? In any case, the document became an important addition to the accumulation of evidence against the ill-omened prince.

History had brought the two forces closer and closer to final conflict. There remained only the question of where it would occur.

19

THE HILL OF THE BELLS

Querétaro
1867

After his brief victory and subsequent defeat at Zaca-tecas, Miramón had retreated to the colonial city of Querétaro, which stood on the central plateau sur-rounded by low hills. The city's tiled church-domes and bell towers were a reminder of its Spanish past. He was joined by Tomás Mejía, an Indian tribal leader, or *cacique*, from the nearby mountains, who had risen to generalship in Maximilian's army.

By now there were fewer than twenty thousand men left in the imperial forces. They were for the most part Mexicans, but there was among them an assortment of Europeans, and even a few veterans of the United States' Army of the Confederacy. About half the troops were defending the three major cities still in imperial control:

Querétaro, Veracruz, and Puebla. The other half were deployed to protect Mexico City.

Maximilian's generals were well aware that theirs was a losing battle. Miramón wrote, philosophically, that the republicans were invincible because they were defending the national cause. Maximilian himself knew the empire was on the brink of collapse.

But the reactionaries in Mexico City still hoped to save themselves with a show of power before the final disaster. They were afraid that Maximilian might abdicate unless he was involved in the field, and so they urged him to assume supreme command and to take the bulk of the local troops to Querétaro, which was even now threatened by the approach of an enormous republican army.

Juárez himself was in the north, in San Luis Potosí. He had recently been approached by Maximilian's agents with another offer of compromise but he had dismissed it, knowing that the whole country would soon be in republican hands. He had decided that the enemy's most vulnerable spot was Querétaro, and while his fellow Oaxacan Díaz marched on the imperial stronghold of Puebla, farther to the south, he had ordered General Mariano Escobedo and two other generals to move toward the low hills surrounding Querétaro.

Slowly, the twenty-seven thousand Juarist forces encircled the city, closing all roads and cutting off supplies of food and water. Then the fighting began.

At first, Maximilian bivouacked with his men on a low hill to the west of the city, called Hill of the Bells. He slept on a blanket, as they did, and earned their admiration for his hardihood and for his bravery in combat. But republican cannon began to threaten the hill and he was forced to move down into the city, into a barracks that had been set up in the convent of a church. Here he was stricken by fever and dysentery and was unable to fight.

February gave way to March, and March was almost over. The imperial command decided that Márquez, the "Tiger of Tacubaya," and the turncoat Vidaurri should try to break through enemy lines with twelve hundred men and make their way to Mexico City for reinforcements. Márquez reached the capital, took on the extra men, but, instead of returning to rescue his besieged emperor, turned toward Puebla, where he was roundly defeated by Porfirio Díaz.

And now it was April. Within the besieged city food and water were all but gone. Late in the month the republicans offered Maximilian a safe-conduct in exchange for the surrender of the city and the imperial army. But Maximilian refused to seek his own safety at the expense of his men, and the siege went on.

In the middle of May, the royalists decided they would make one last attempt to break through the encircling republican forces. But on the night preceding the planned breakthrough, a colonel named Miguel López, whom Maximilian had befriended, made plans of his own. He accepted a bribe from the besiegers to remove the guard and let the republican forces into the city. He stipulated only that the emperor be given an opportunity to escape.

At three in the morning, the republican forces were admitted. They made their way silently through the dark streets as far as imperial headquarters. There was sudden, brief confusion. Miramón was wounded in the face. And somehow or other Maximilian, who was given his chance to escape, did not take it. Instead, he and General Mejía managed to reach the Hill of the Bells, still prepared for combat. They were surrounded and taken prisoner. By dawn, all the bells in all the bell towers of Querétaro were sounding, to proclaim the republican victory.

Imprisoned, Maximilian conducted himself with dignity. He informed General Mariano Escobedo that he wished to be the only victim, if a sacrifice were required; and he asked that he and his two generals, Mejía and the wounded Miramón, be allowed to leave Mexico, never to return. Escobeda relayed the request to the president, in San Luis Potosí.

But Juárez's decision had been formed even before the message reached him. On May 15, just before the dispatch arrived telling him of the fall of Querétaro, he had been writing a letter to his family in which he said: "The government . . . makes haste slowly, with the firm determination to do what best befits the country, and without being influenced in its decisions by personal vengeance, misguided compassion, or any foreign threat. We have fought for the independence and autonomy of Mexico, and it must be a reality." It was necessary to prove before the whole world that Mexican soil must never again be intruded upon by a foreign aggressor. In answer to the news of Querétaro's fall and the capture of the imperial leaders, he sent back orders that Maximilian, Miramón and Mejía be tried by court-martial. It was the same fate Maximilian had decreed for republican leaders had they been defeated and captured.

The captive emperor then appealed for a personal interview with Juárez, thinking perhaps that when the president understood the purity of his motives all would be forgiven. But Juárez sensed the danger in an appeal to his sentiments and answered that Maximilian could say whatever he had to say at the court-martial.

It was the second week in June. There being no other suitable site in Querétaro for the trial, it was held in a theater. The spectators watched from below and the principals—the defense, their three able lawyers from Mexico City, the prosecution, and the presiding officers— enacted their roles onstage. Mejía and the wounded Miramón were present, but Maximilian remained in his prison cell, refusing to submit himself to the humiliation of such an appearance.

The proceedings lasted for four days. The three defense attorneys contended that Maximilian and his supporters had acted only for the good of the nation. The prosecution presented in evidence Maximilian's "Black decree" of April 1865, which had ordered the execution of many republican leaders. Indeed, he was held guilty for all the casualties since the French army had withdrawn.

When the hearings went to a vote, the inevitable conclusion was reached. Three of the presiding officers voted for Maximilian's banishment, and four for his death. Miramón and Mejía received the same sentence.

While the three prisoners waited for the hour of execution in their cells in Querétaro, a flood of letters, telegrams, and personal pleas for clemency poured into Juárez's headquarters in San Luis Potosí. There were messages from half the crowned heads of Europe, and from Secretary of State Seward of the United States. There was even a plea from the revolutionary Giuseppe Garibaldi of Italy, who had long proclaimed the Juarist cause abroad. Victor Hugo, still bitterly anti-Bonaparte, wrote urging Juárez to spare Maximilian's life and abolish the death penalty from the face of the earth.

Miramón's wife and two small children appeared before the president, adding their pleas to the others. The most colorful visitor was the Princess Agnes Salm-Salm, an American circus acrobat who had married a titled adventurer now imprisoned with Maximilian. She forced her way into Juárez's private office and threw herself on her knees to beg for the emperor's life. Juárez, who was deeply embarrassed by the scene, said, "If all the kings and queens of Europe were at your side, I could not spare his life."

In the end, Juárez went into seclusion for three days and refused to see anyone. It had been an ordeal for him, too, to appear before the world as merciless and vengeful. But he had written his last word on the subject: "The government acts by necessity on this occasion, denying humanitarian sentiments. . . . The law and the sentence are inexorable now, because public safety so demands."

In his cell in Querétaro, Maximilian was calm, conducting himself with quiet dignity. Like Shakespeare's Thane of Cawdor, ". . . Nothing in his life / Became him like the leaving it." He wrote affectionate letters to his family and a tender one to Carlota, if by chance she were well enough to read it. To those about him he spoke no word of bitterness. The day before his execution he made one more appeal that his two comrades be spared and that he be the only one to die. And he wired Juárez, urging that his own blood be the last shed, that it might serve to reconcile all Mexicans and bring peace to the unhappy country.

The following day, June 19, at dawn, the emperor, Miramón, and Mejía were taken by carriage to the Hill of the Bells, where Maximilian had been captured. Four thousand armed men stood guard. Maximilian recognized and greeted several old friends among the spectators, and gave his forgiveness to the captain of the firing squad. Allowed a few last words, he said, "I die for a just cause, the cause of the freedom and independence of Mexico. May my blood put an end to the misfortunes of my new country. *Viva México!*"

The spray of bullets did not kill him at once. His last word, as he lay in terrible pain on the ground, was in the language of his adopted Mexico. *"Hombre . . . !"* he cried. "Man . . . !"

Two days after the emperor's death, Mexico City fell to Porfirio Díaz. Márquez eluded capture and escaped to Havana, where he became a pawnbroker. Vidaurri was shot as a traitor, as were two other imperial generals. Otherwise, Maximilian's plea that his blood be the last to be shed proved prophetic. There were no further executions.

Across the ocean, in Belgium, Carlota lived on in her dream world. No one told her what had happened to her husband. She went on speaking of him, until the day she died, as "Sovereign of the Universe."

It was midsummer now, and rains poured down on the central plateau and on the valley of Mexico. Juárez's old black carriage made its painful way along flooded and washed-out roads, stopping frequently for repairs before it reached Chapultepec. There the mud was washed off, but the bullet holes in it could not be obliterated. Two days later, on July 15, 1867, it bore Juárez on his formal entry into the heart of the city.

Bands played, cannon sounded. Spectators in the

zócalo cheered themselves hoarse, and rockets burst in the sky. Three little girls presented Juárez with a crown of flowers, but inadvertently placed it on his head back-to-front, so the ribbons dangled down over his face.

It was Juárez himself, divested of the wreath, who raised the flag once more over the National Palace, as he had lowered it that sorry evening more than five years before. A brave and enormous banner of green, white and red, it fluttered high overhead, its eagle and serpent glinting brilliantly in the high clear air.

A few days earlier, the U.S. revenue cutter *Wilderness,* out of New Orleans, had reached the wind-whipped waters of Veracruz, and Margarita Juárez and her family had come ashore, bringing with them the bodies of Pepito and the baby Antonio to be buried in Mexican soil. In the midst of the summer storms, the group set out by coach to travel over the rain-pitted and war-ravaged roads, up out of the tropics to the highlands, past the tiled domes of Peubla and the pyramids and churches of Cholula to Mexico City which they reached on July 25.

The Juárez family was together again at last.

20

THE LAST CHAPTER

Mexico City
1867-1872

Two years earlier, when the Civil War ended and a pistol shot had fatally wounded the president of the United States at Ford's Theater in Washington, Lincoln had been at the peak of his achievement. It was his tragedy to be cut down at that moment. But his image would survive untarnished in his country's history. His successors Andrew Johnson and Ulysses S. Grant would have to bear the bitterness and recriminations that followed the war's end.

The raising of the flag over Mexico's National Palace in 1867 was Juárez's supreme moment. His tragedy was to live beyond it.

The great issue of national survival had vanished, and in its place came countless smaller ones, raising disagreement and dissension. People who for ten years had idolized Juárez as the very spirit of the nation now began to find fault with him. In part it was because he was a convenient scapegoat for the country's problems. And as Juárez well knew, there were many. "When a society like ours," he said, "has had the misfortune to pass through years of intense upheaval, it is seamed through with vices whose profound roots cannot be extirpated either in a single day or by any single measure."

Mexico was three hundred million pesos in debt. She had almost no foreign trade, save with her near neighbors, and there was a grave danger she might become all too dependent on American capital. Also, while the middle and upper classes had profited from the forced sale of church and *ejidal* land in the years since the Reform, the poor had not. The condition of the peon was as hopeless as ever.

And the majority of the nation's inhabitants were still illiterate. They could be herded into polling places in the rural villages and handed a prepared ballot, and the results would be a foregone conclusion. The opposition could, and usually did, cry fraud. One of Juárez's first acts, therefore, was to decree free and compulsory education for every child in Mexico.

But there was a difference between declaring a law and turning it into fact. The country lacked trained teachers and money to build schools. Five years later there would still be only 350,000 children in school, out of a school-age population of two million.

In addition, the country found itself with an enormous

army, whose maintenance cost almost half the national budget. In a desperate economy move, Juárez dismissed forty thousand soldiers, creating an enormous body of unemployed—and bitter—veterans, many of whom swelled the ranks in subsequent uprisings. Others turned to crime, and Mexico was swept by an unprecedented wave of murders and armed robberies.

Juárez's closest adviser during this period was the brilliant Sebastian Lerdo de Tejada, a younger brother of the author of the Lerdo law which had set the Reform in motion ten years before. For secretary of treasury he brought home from the United States his trusted ambassador Matías Romero, who did manage to establish some sort of economic stability for the impoverished country.

Juárez's most visible, and concrete, accomplishment was the building of a railroad from Mexico City to Veracruz. As he had realized when he was governor of Oaxaca, schools matter little to an impoverished people. A more immediate need, he knew, was a means by which their produce could be transported from the mines and farms of the hinterlands to seaports, and from there abroad or to other parts of the country.

The railroad, when it was completed a year after his death, was a masterpiece of engineering and construction, skirting mountain precipices, crossing abysses hundreds of feet deep, and descending by careful stages from the pine-covered mountains surrounding the valley of

Mexico down to the tropical greens of the coast. It was in itself a monument to the man who had initiated it.

But there was so much else to be done for the country, and so little time in which to do it! In 1870 Juárez suffered a stroke, and though he recovered completely, it may have served to warn him that his useful years were limited. Whatever was to be accomplished must be done quickly.

In any event, the quiet patience for which he had been famous seemed to be wearing thin. As though he found Congress's arguments and delays intolerably irksome, he frequently bypassed it, or requested powers not granted him by the constitution. He had become accustomed to extraordinary powers during wartime, and now it seemed more efficient to go on functioning in the same direct way.

But Congress was jealous of its power. It was a time when egos flourished and tempers ran short, when arguments on the floor went on for months. In and out of Congress, ambitious men were struggling to make names for themselves. The general from Oaxaca, Porfirio Díaz, had been defeated by Juárez in the 1867 elections, but everyone knew he was only biding his time until the aging president should make a misstep.

It came in 1871, when Juárez ran for a fourth term as president.

The previous year, Juárez had had one somber satisfaction. In midsummer of 1870, the Prussian leader Bismarck had maneuvered Napoleon III into a war. Napo-leon had squandered so many men and so much money on the Mexican intervention that he had little left to fight with, and was at last receiving a liberal dose of his own medicine. By summer's end he and one hundred thou-sand men surrendered at Sedan. As a French newspaper commented later, with considerable bitterness, "We should not have lost Alsace and Lorraine if we had had a Juárez!"

But later in the year, Juárez's attention had turned from war and politics to something much closer to his heart: the health of his *viejecita*.

Margarita had been painfully, and seriously, ill for some time. Christmas that year, in their small house next to the church of San Cosme, could have brought little joy to any of the Juárez family. It must have been only one more unhappy day of waiting.

Margarita was forty-four years old, twenty years younger than Juárez. In all their years together neither of them could have thought that she might die first. But, gently born and bred by the well-to-do Mazas, since her marriage she had been three times a refugee. She had taken her family on foot through summer's heat and rains, hundreds of miles across the mountains to join Juárez in Veracruz. And later, living without him in a vast city where she could not even speak the language, she had watched two beloved sons die. In earlier years, she had also lost three other children, but at least, when they had died, Juárez had been at her side, and had helped her bear the sorrow.

Perhaps it had all been too much hardship, too much grief. On the second day of the new year, 1871, she died.

The day afterward, Juárez was able to summon the strength to lift her into her coffin, but he could do no more. He left it for others to close the coffin and bear it out into the street. Two of the pallbearers were men who had led recent uprisings, but Juárez had pardoned them, and now they performed this last service for him.

He had invited no one to the funeral, but all along the route to the *pantheon*, vast crowds appeared, black-garbed, standing silently as the procession went by, in tribute to a woman so self-effacing, as one historian has said, that she was noticed only when she died.

For almost a month, Juárez was unable to work. And for a brief time, out of respect for his grief, newspapers refrained from attacking him.

But they were soon criticizing him again, as bitterly as ever. Unlike the government of Porfirio Díaz, whose dictatorship followed close on the heels of Juárez's death and which lasted for thirty years, Juárez's government allowed complete freedom of expression, and the opposition took full advantage of it.

In the meantime, in spite of an unfriendly press and sporadic uprisings here and there about the countryside, Juárez decided to run for reelection. And now his critics became truly vitriolic.

Even his friends may well have wondered why he chose to run. He was sixty-five years old and still in mourning for his wife. Surely it was time he retired, to rest on his past accomplishments! Surely he must have had honor enough from his countrymen, during his thirteen years as president.

But that was precisely the point. Juárez had devoted his whole life to the service of Mexico, and it would be hard for him to conceive of any other sort of life. It is also possible, as his critics charged, that he *had* come to think of himself as indispensable to the nation's welfare. Certainly, the country was fraught with problems he could not easily dismiss.

And who was there to take his place? Lerdo de Tejada had been building himself a following, the last few years, but they were primarily wealthy men, landowners, and bureaucrats. As for the third candidate, general Porfirio Díaz, he was little more than a selfish and ambitious military leader, eager for power. He might—and, as events proved, *did*—put an end to Mexico's hard-won democracy. Juárez undoubtedly felt he could not entrust the nation's future to either man. Whatever his motives, he decided to ignore his critics, and to run once more for the presidency.

The voters went to the polls in July, but the count was not completed until August. Juárez led Díaz and Tejada, but did not have a majority, and by law the election had to be decided in the legislature. Congress voted overwhelmingly for Juárez.

Porfirio Díaz and his brother protested that the elections had been a fraud. They initiated a rebellion in Oaxaca, which the army put down by force. Díaz fled into the mountains, to bide his time once more. On the first of December, 1871, Juárez was sworn into office, with Lerdo de Tejada as his chief justice and successor.

The winter of 1871 to 1872 ended, like other winters, except that for the aging Juárez it was the loneliest he had known. Then came *primavera*, the "first truth," springtime, dry and windy, as spring always was in the valley of Mexico. Dust blew from the drying lakebed of Texcoco, parching the lips and making the eyes smart. Dead leaves swirled from the trees and skittered along the cobbled streets. Clouds formed above the mountains and swept across the sky, but gave no rain. People began to yearn for the first thunder, the first wet drops that heralded the rainy season.

It was on such a spring day that Juárez received a delegation of orphans in the National Palace. Funds for their orphanage had been cut off. He had been paying for their food and lodging out of his own pocket, and they had come to thank him. As he was giving them each a peso to buy fruit, he suddenly turned pale, and his hand went to his heart.

But the pain diminished. Time had given him another reprieve. He finished the interview and, when the children had gone, went on with more serious business.

The rains came. The trees in the zócalo and along the

Alameda were covered with pale green buds. Juárez worked daily at the National Palace, ignoring the unrelenting charges in the newspapers that he had outlived his time. Who knows? Perhaps he had. "We are in full retrogression," thundered one journalist. ". . . Don Benito Juárez is the Messiah of the owls and the crows. He is moving backward with giant strides. He is returning to the past. . . ."

On the morning of July 18, his physician was called. He found that the president was suffering successive attacks of angina pectoris. As each pain receded, however, Juárez insisted on getting up, until the next pain forced him back to his bed again.

After several hours, his heart began to fail. Dr. Alvarez tried the desperate measure used in Mexico in those days. He poured boiling water directly onto Juárez's bare chest.

Apparently the remedy was effective, because Juárez seemed to revive, and was soon sitting up in his chair again. His family, reassured, went to dinner. When he and the doctor were alone, Juárez began to reminisce about his boyhood, about the Maza family, and the old bookbinder don Salanueva, who had educated him. At one point he interrupted himself to ask:

"Doctor, is my illness mortal?"

The doctor nodded. Without a change of expression, Juárez continued his boyhood stories until another and still stronger attack felled him. Once more the boiling water was applied, and Juárez bore it without complaint.

He revived enough to return to his chair and receive several government officials. He gave them no hint that he was suffering from anything more serious than rheumatism.

Later, when he seemed to be sleeping, the doctor and his family left him. Just before midnight, he died.

Soon after they found him in his last sleep, a death mask was made of his face. It preserves forever the expression he wore in that last hour, an expression of ineffable sweetness. It is not the stern face of a nation's president, but the gentle, kindly face of an affectionate father, with the faintest touch of a smile on the lips.

"The little Indian's" long, hard journey, begun that early morning when he had crept out of his sleeping village and started down the mountain in search of an education, was over. In the years since, he had not ever, even for a moment, forgotten the people he had sprung from, nor the soil which had given him birth.

GLOSSARY

abrazo: a friendly embrace

cacique: chieftain or "strong man" of a rural area

café con leche: coffee with milk

calzones: trousers, particularly those of unbleached muslin worn by the Indians

campesino: small farmer

centavo: coin worth about a penny

comida: midday dinner

conquistador: conqueror (usually referring to the Spaniards at the time of the Conquest)

Creole: a person of Spanish blood but born in Latin America

diputado: a delegate to Congress

ejido: commons, village-owned land for the use of small farmers *fueros*: privileges exempt from civil law

grito: a cry, specifically Father Hidalgo's when he proclaimed Mexico's independence

hacendado: owner of an hacienda

hacienda: a large, self-sustaining ranch

hombre: man

ley: law

licenciado: lawyer

maestro: teacher or master

mestizo: of mixed Indian and Spanish parentage

norte: north. N.: north wind

padre: father or priest

panadero: baker

pantheon: cemetery

Pascua: Easter

peon: the poorest day-laborer, usually attached to an hacienda like a serf

peso: in the mid-1800s, worth about a dollar

petate: woven straw mat, used variously as rug, bed, or protection from the rain

rancho: ranch

rebozo: shawl

sala: parlor

sierra: mountain range

tierra caliente: hot lands, tropics

viejecita: little old woman

zócalo: main plaza

SOURCES

I am indebted to the late Ralph Roeder and his perceptive and beautiful *Juárez and His Mexico* for many of his insights into the period of Juárez, as well as for his translations from original texts, and his kindness in letting me excerpt from them.

The quote on page 16 is taken from Helen Augur's book *Zapotec*.

The historian referred to on page 169 is Ralph Roeder.

In general, the data in this book are based on information—and sometimes observations—from the following sources:

AUGUR, HELEN, *Zapotec*. Dolphin Books, Garden City, New York: Doubleday & Co., 1954.

CALDERON DE LA BARCA, FANNY. *Life in Mexico*. Edited by Howard T. and Marion Hall Fisher. Garden City, New York: Doubleday & Co., 1966.

GRUENING, ERNEST. *Mexico and Its Heritage*. New York: Appleton-Century-Crofts, 1928.

MORRIS, RICHARD B., ed. *Encyclopedia of American History*. New York: Harper & Brothers, 1953.

PARKES, HENRY BAMFORD. *A History of Mexico*. Cambridge, Mass.: Houghton Mifflin Co., 1950.

ROEDER, RALPH. *Juárez and His Mexico*. New York: The Viking Press, 1947.

SANDBURG, CARL. *Abraham Lincoln; The Prairie Years*. New York: Harcourt, Brace & Co., 1926.

SMART, CHARLES ALLEN. *Viva Juárez!* Philadelphia and New York: J. B. Lippincott Co., 1963.

TERRY, T. PHILIP. *Terry's Guide to Mexico*. Boston and Hingham, Mass.: 1938.

WOODWARD, WM. *A New American History*, Garden City, New York: Garden City Publishing Co., 1938.

NOTE: Those interested in Maximilian's role in Mexico's history might also enjoy *Phantom Crown*, by Bertita Harding (New York: E. P. Dutton & Co., 1960).

INDEX